Indian

Ocean

Legs 3 & 4
At back of book

AUSTRALIA

Leg Two
Cape Town to Auckland
Restart: 12/5/98
Distance: 6,884 N.M.

Auckland

ZEALAND

60°   75°   90°   105°   120°   135°   150°   165°   180°

into the wind

Around Alone: The story of the world's longest race

into the wind

Around Alone: The story of the world's longest race

TONY BARTELME & BRIAN HICKS

EVENING POST PUBLISHING COMPANY
Charleston, South Carolina, USA

Edited by Steve Mullins
Design by Gill Guerry

Printed and bound in The USA
by The R.L. Bryan Company

Library of Congress Cataloguing-in-Publication Data

Bartelme, Tony and Hicks, Brian
    Into The Wind
            Around Alone: The story of the world's longest race/
    Tony Bartelme and Brian Hicks

    ISBN 0-934-870-94-2

    1. Yacht racing. 2. Sailing, singlehanded. 3. Around Alone
    race. I. Title.

                                                    99-71145
                                                      CIP

FIRST EDITION
0 9 8 7 6 5 4 3 2 1

For Luke and Cole

THE SAILORS

Class I

Entrant	Yacht Name	Nationality
Isabelle Autissier	PRB	France
Mike Golding	Team Group 4	UK
Josh Hall	Gartmore Investment Management	UK
Fedor Konioukhov	Modern University for the Humanities	Russia
Sebastian Reidl	Project Amazon	Canada
Giovanni Soldini	FILA	Italy
Marc Thiercelin	SOMEWHERE	France

Class II

Entrant	Yacht Name	Nationality
Robin Davie	South Carolina	UK
Michael Garside	Magellan Alpha	UK
Neil Hunter	Paladin II	Australia
Brad Van Liew	Balance Bar	USA
Jean-Pierre Mouligne	Cray Valley	France
Neal Petersen	www.no-barriers.com	South Africa
Minoru Saito	Shuten-dohji II	Japan
George Stricker	Rapscallion III	USA
Viktor Yazykov	Wind of Change-Russia	Russia

CONTENTS

PREFACE

In 1982, a small fleet of sailboats - each boat manned by a single skipper - left Newport, Rhode Island, on a grueling race through the world's most dangerous and lonely seas. Called The BOC Challenge, the race spawned stories of courage, tragedy, and triumph.

Seventeen years and four races later, the event's basic rules have remained the same: One sailor per boat; three stops; and two divisions - Class One for boats 51- to 60 feet long and Class Two for boats 40 to 50 feet in length.

The race, however, has seen its share of changes. Its home port is now Charleston, South Carolina, and it has a new name: Around Alone. On a deeper level, the race has evolved into a laboratory for a new and controversial breed of sailing vessels capable of reaching incredible speeds. And, because of the marriage of Internet and satellite technology, the Around Alone also has given the world a new window into the minds of those who dare to push the limits of their physical and mental endurance.

When, in the autumn of 1998, sixteen solo skippers left Charleston on the race's fifth edition, thousands of armchair sailors went with them, monitoring their progress, moods, and experiences on the Web and in the daily pages of newspapers like The (Charleston) *Post and Courier*. As in the previous four races, we were witness to unforgettable sea stories. This book is an attempt to chronicle these tales and the intriguing people behind them.

Ready to Race

CHAPTER ONE

You are on a fast boat.

Alone.

From behind, a huge gray wave the size of a building rolls toward you. You're flying now, twenty knots or so, generating a wide white wake. But these waves are faster. And they soon catch up.

Hold on!

If you had a crew, that's what they would yell. But you're alone, and no one has to tell you to get a grip. Your muscles are always tense; you always have one hand on something. You're part of this boat. Now, the bow is lifting, pointing toward the sky, and your boat is still screaming, up, up, up the wave. And then you're at the crest, and you can see an endless series of green and gray mounds marching toward the horizon. The wind howls so loud it feels as if someone is ripping paper inside your ears. And now, down this roller coaster, picking up speed, pushed by the wind, pulled by gravity, a nine-ton surfboard ...twenty-two knots ...twenty-five knots. The water rushes along the deck like a wild mountain rapid ... twenty-eight knots ... thirty knots. You feel the drop in your stomach. You hear every creak and groan the boat makes, the whistle of the winds through the rigging. Sometimes you make deals with the mast, the boom, the forestay, the shrouds. "Don't break,

and I'll be good to you." You know that if the boat steers the wrong way down this wave you could pitch-pole, but the autopilot works well this time, and your course is true. You brace for the impact because it can knock the wind out of you. Then you're in the trough and the bow slices into the back of the next wave and is buried by a mass of white spray and bubbles, and suddenly the water is everywhere and the air feels as if it's full of needles, but you forget all that, you forget that your hands are frozen by the thirty-eight-degree water boiling around you, and you think for a split second, yeah, this is no dream, this is life, raw and real.

Under an awakening sun, far from the rollicking, roller coaster oceans circling the Antarctic, Isabelle Autissier left her apartment in suburban Mount Pleasant and sped toward the bridge to downtown Charleston. The day was September 26, 1998. In the morning light, the old steel bridges hung like a giant piece of gray lace over the Cooper River. As she reached the top of the span, 150 feet over the river's glass-smooth waters, she could see Fort Sumter in the distance, where the Civil War began, and the jetties protecting the mouth of Charleston Harbor. Just beyond the jetties was the starting line for the

Around Alone.

This would be the fourth time Autissier had entered a solo around-the-world race. It probably would be her last. For ten years she had sailed the world's most isolated and dangerous oceans. She had already told several friends that she might retire after this race - try to end her storied singlehanded sailing career by becoming the first woman to win such an event.

The press dubbed her the odds-on favorite, and the media's confidence matched her own. Her crew had prepared the boat

beautifully. She knew the world's currents and winds as well as anyone in the fleet. Several other skippers had newer boats, but she had more time on the water with hers and knew the sounds it made when something was about to break or tear. She was ready to race. But first she had to get through the next few hours.

She hated teary goodbyes. She also knew that she would be in the spotlight, not her favorite place. All those journalists hovering about like seagulls, pecking at her for a quote or a sound bite. Oh well, she was used to it. Public relations, marketing and the media were as much a part of the race as the wind. Indeed, she needed them all. They had made her a worldwide celebrity, bestowed the kind of fame that made it easy to attract sponsors to help pay for her sailing adventures. She would patiently feed the flock.

It was a still, warm morning. When she arrived at the Charleston Maritime Center the docks were jammed with skippers and their shore crews busy saying goodbye or making last-minute repairs. Autissier was one of sixteen sailors entered in the race. She walked down the Maritime Center's concrete pier to an aluminum gangway. Below, like an old friend, was her boat *PRB*.

It wasn't the flashiest yacht in the fleet, but it was a proven speed machine. Shaped like a giant white arrowhead, the carbon fiber hull lay low and flat in the water. Everything was designed to use the wind or let the boat slip through it more easily. Behind the mast, a bulbous cabin emerged ever-so-slightly from the deck. The mast itself was eighty-six feet tall, able to carry 3,000 square feet of sail. Surfing down a wave, the boat could top thirty knots. It was her boat, and hers alone. The designers configured the cabin to match her height and the length of her legs. She built it in 1996 and had already sailed it in another round-the-world race, the Vendee Globe.

Unlike the Around Alone, which has three stops, the Vendee is a nonstop race. Autissier was in second place when debris sheared off one of her two rudders. When she ducked into

South Africa for repairs, she was disqualified. After fixing the rudder, she sailed on anyway, completing the circumnavigation in 105 days. Unofficially, she finished second, not far behind the winner, Christophe Auguin.

Except for the rudder problem, the boat had proven tough, fast and dependable. In the Southern Pacific, storms knocked the yacht on its side more than five times. Like a prizefighter, the boat slowly came back up after each blow. Some of her rivals weren't so lucky. Several boats ended belly-up. One crash took the life of her friend, Gerry Roufs. When he sent a distress call, she was 150 miles downwind. She turned into the wind and searched for him in storms so violent she couldn't tell the sea from the skies. She broke a finger. Her mainsail was torn. "It's war out here," she said in a message faxed to her shore team. "I am at my last physical limits." Forty-foot waves rolling along at twenty-five knots tossed her boat. After a punishing day, rescue officials released her from the search. She continued to crisscross the area for hours anyway without any luck. "I will never forget those conditions," she would say a year later in a symposium on the safety of singlehanded racing yachts. "All round-the-world boats can capsize."

Standing next to *PRB* the morning of the Around Alone start, Autissier seemed an unlikely sports celebrity. She was forty-one years old and not particularly muscular, though her hands and forearms were sinewy and hard. She was clad in a green polo-type shirt with a patch on the front identifying her sponsor. She wore long blue pants. Two large, round earrings dangled from her ears, and sunglasses hung from her neck. Her hair was short, framing a strong nose, soft blue eyes, and on this day, a business-like smile when someone handed her a bouquet of flowers. She was used to the attention, the requests for autographs, the pointing fingers. As the only woman in a race, she was a magnet for the press. Before she started racing, long-distance singlehanded yachting was a mostly male domain. Now, in France, she has become a household name. Once on a Paris subway, a girl came up to her and said, "Aren't you the sailor who likes earrings?" Autissier smiled and said, "I suppose so." Then the girl took off her earrings and handed them to her. Autissier was so moved she

wore them on the start of the 1996 Vendee Globe.

The sea, not fame, had always been her compass, though. The fourth of five daughters, she grew up in Paris. Her father was an architect who taught her how to sail at age six during family holidays to the coast of Brittany. Fascinated by the wind and waves and creatures living in them, she eventually became a marine researcher. In the late 1980s, she took up singlehanded sailing "for self-improvement," and in 1990, she quit her job as a scientist to sail full-time, entering the BOC Challenge, (renamed the Around Alone for the 1998-99 race). Despite losing her mast midway, she finished the race in seventh place, becoming the first woman to complete a round-the-world singlehanded race.

In doing so, she joined a tiny fraternity of offshore ocean racers. Fewer than one hundred singlehanded skippers have made the deadly 27,000-mile journey. Around Alone race officials liked to point out that more people have circled the globe in space. Since the first round-the-world race, the 1968 Golden Globe, five singlehanded racers have died, two in the four Around Alone races. Many more watched waves shred their masts, rudders and keels. These mishaps often triggered daring rescues and international headlines. In the 1994-95 race, Autissier lost her mast in a violent Indian Ocean storm. She fashioned a makeshift rig and sailed to the Kerguelen Islands, a remote island chain with a French weather station. There, she installed a new mast and set off again - only to be caught in another storm. A huge rogue wave picked up her yacht and threw it forward and upside down, smashing the cabin roof and wiping away her rig. Autissier was down below when it happened and would have been washed into the near-freezing waters had she not been crouched in a compartment, checking some gear. Four days later, an Australian military helicopter airlifted her to safety in an expensive rescue that prompted some to question whether singlehanded sailing needlessly endangers both the skippers and those dispatched to save them. Autissier, however, also was praised for her cool, fearless manner during

the entire episode.

Now, four years later, standing on the deck of *PRB* (short for her sponsor, Produits de Revetment du Batiment), Autissier showed her usual poise. While anxious shore crew, media and friends spun around her, she was calm and contained, like a hurricane's eye. A reporter approached and asked if she was worried about the tropical storms churning north through the Atlantic. No, she said, they wouldn't be a big factor.

Was she ready?

"I am quite happy to go because the boat is ready," she said in a tone that sounded as if she had recited the same words a dozen times that morning. "It is hard to say goodbye, but it is a relief to be on the water."

Another skipper, Giovanni Soldini, walked up and gave her

INTO THE WIND

a bon voyage gift: a bag of pasta. She smiled and gave him a hug. They told each other to be careful. "Come back to Charleston," Autissier told her friend.

Soldini also was a member of the round-the-world racing fraternity. In the 1994-95 race, he sailed in a fifty-footer called *Kodak*, built by recovering drug addicts in Italy. He placed second in the Class Two division for forty- to fifty-foot boats and had since become Italy's most famous singlehanded sailor. During that race, Autissier and Soldini became close friends. The two later sailed together in the 1996 BMW per Due, a 535-mile double-handed race in the Mediterranean, claiming first place.

Soldini seemed an even more unlikely sports star than Autissier. Short and thin with a wide stance well-suited for scrambling around a rocking boat, he wore shorts and a blue shirt that seemed a little large and draped down his shoulders. He had several days growth of beard and his longish brown hair seemed to have missed its morning appointment with a comb. With his friends and family around, he was quick to smile, and punctuated the ends of his sentences with squeaky but endearing laughs. As the morning wore on, though, his mood became more somber and serious. He sat alone with his three-year-old daughter, Martina, a bundle of blonde curls and energy. He stared off into the distance for a few minutes, lost in thought.

It had been a painful journey to the starting line. He and his friends had built a new sixty-foot carbon fiber boat, *FILA*, bankrolled by the Italian shoe and apparel company. Like Autissier's *PRB*, Soldini's *FILA* was designed by Groupe Finot in France, the world's leading architect of singlehanded sailing monohulls. It was wide and low, like *PRB*, and also had a swinging keel. During the summer, Soldini and three friends set off from New York toward England, trying to break the record for the fastest crossing by a monohull sailboat. Their new boat performed brilliantly, flying across the Atlantic at a breathtaking pace, gunwale buried in the water, sometimes hit-

A powerful storm had developed 400 miles off the coast of England with 80-mph winds and 65-foot waves. A huge wave rolled the boat and ripped off the mast. Soldini was down below at the time, but his friends, Andrea Romanelli and Andrea Tarlarini, were outside in the cockpit. Tarlarini managed to scramble aboard, but Romanelli was swept overboard and drowned in the swells and spray. The disaster prompted critics to charge that boats like *FILA* were dangerous. These complaints stung Soldini. He felt the boat had performed well in the storm. With its special tilting keel, he had been able to right *FILA* after it capsized and then make it to France without any help. That storm would have devastated other types of boats, he thought. Nevertheless, he felt guilt over the loss of Romanelli, a longtime friend and the yacht's co-designer. Soldini questioned his abilities and whether he should do the Around Alone.

When *FILA* limped into France, Autissier was there to meet him.

"That's the way it is for people who go to sea," she told him. "You have to keep sailing."

The more he thought about it, the more he focused on all the work he and his friends had put into his yacht. It would dishonor Romanelli's memory if he quit. So Soldini and his crew fixed *FILA*, replacing the mast with a stronger one. He entered the Atlantic Alone, a feeder race from Europe to Charleston, and crossed in the record time of 21 days and 17 hours, finishing days ahead of his competition.

As he paced on his deck the morning of the Around Alone start, Soldini thought about Romanelli. He felt all the energy his friend had put into the boat's design and construction. He vowed to win the race for his friend and others who had stayed by his side all these years. It was time to go now. He picked up his daughter one last time and gave her a hug. Then he walked away from his shore crew and family to the boat's bow. He put one foot on the bowsprit, rested his elbow on his knee, stroked his beard, and gazed out to sea.

ting thirty-five knots or more. As they approached Europe, the only thing between them and the record was a giant wall of wind.

Sixteen Adventurers

Robin Davie paced the docks, pressing a cellular phone to his ear and cursing between drags on his cigarette. His boat's alternator was still on the blink, and the race was just about to start.

Since the first race in 1982, the Around Alone has attracted a diverse group of adventurers, dreamers, and professional sailors, and Davie was all of them wrapped into a nicotine-craving whirlwind of a man. A wiry Brit, he had deep sun-lines in his face and black hair with sun-bleached streaks of gray. His language was salty enough to cure a side of beef. Like Autissier and Soldini, Davie was an Around Alone veteran. He first dreamed of sailing around the world when he was a teenager. When he was old enough, he joined the British merchant marine, later spending two years with the British military in its war with Argentina over the Falkland Islands. In the mid-1980s, he worked with a company that salvaged tankers destroyed in Iran's war with Iraq. He was aboard two tankers when they were hit with missiles. It was dangerous work, but the pay was good, and he saved enough money to buy a yacht and compete in the 1990 race. He raced again in 1994, but was so exhausted when he finished that he stayed in Charleston for a few months to rest. He eventually got married and made the city his permanent home, hoping to land an American sponsor

willing to shell out the money for a fast sixty-footer. He didn't have any luck finding a big boat but managed to persuade Windex Yachts of Great Britain to lend him a fifty-foot prototype. He renamed the boat *South Carolina* and spent nearly a year refitting it. But with three hours to go before the noon start, he still wasn't finished with all the repairs and modifications.

"It's looking tight for the start," he barked into the cell

Robin Davie on *South Carolina*

enough money to retire and sail full time. His goal was to become the first Japanese man to circumnavigate the globe alone three times. In his heavy fifty-footer, he had no chance of winning, but he would give the other slow boats a run for their money, he vowed. "This time - not last boat," he told a spectator as he wrestled with some lines.

Across the docks, a priest blessed Russian skipper Fedor Konioukhov and his boat, *Modern University for the Humanities*. Konioukhov was one of Russia's most famous adventurers. He had climbed the highest mountains on all seven continents, including Mount Everest, and skied to the North and South poles. He had already sailed around the world twice, but this was his first race. Winning was not his goal. Rather, he hoped to gather ideas for his art. He was a well-known painter in Moscow. During the race, he also would study for a law degree. It was part of an experiment by his sponsor, a large Russian university, to determine whether it was possible to study in extreme conditions. If he returned to Charleston, he would receive a diploma.

At first glance, Konioukhov looked more like a hippie than a world-class mountaineer and adventurer. A thick, scraggly brown beard danced across his face. His hair was long, and he had a shy smile. But he was thin and strong like a marathoner, and his eyes had the confident and tranquil gaze of someone comfortable with a challenge.

After the priest's blessing, Konioukhov walked over to Giovanni Soldini's yacht and gave him a bon voyage bottle of vodka. A few yards away, Sebastian Reidl, a gold prospector from Canada, was saying his goodbyes. With his white beard and assured smile, Reidl resembled a plump Sean Connery. His two-masted yacht, *Project Amazon*, named to bring attention to the destruction of the South American rain forest, was the

phone.

Near Davie's boat was Minoru Saito's yacht, *Shuten-dohji II*. At sixty-four, Saito was the oldest skipper in the fleet. Like Davie, he had done the race twice before, finishing in last place in the 1994-95 event. Unlike Davie, he had a serious heart condition. Stashed on board was a full complement of heart and blood pressure pills, plus some Scotch to wash them all down. Saito had managed a gas station in Tokyo and invested in the Japanese stock market in the 1960s, saving

Fedor Konioukhov on start day

Sebastian Reidl

black hair and wide darting eyes, Petersen had overcome a crippling hip condition as a child to become a professional diamond diver and sailor. He had the smallest boat in the fleet, a yacht he built himself a decade earlier, during the days of apartheid. Petersen hoped to become the first black person to race around the world alone.

The cast of characters also included J.P. Mouligne, a former professional knife-thrower, and Mike Garside, a magazine publisher and former officer in the British Special Forces fond of telling reporters how much he despised sailing. Two Americans were in the race: Brad Van Liew, who ran an airplane management company in California catering in part to Hollywood stars, and George Stricker, an ex-Marine and entrepreneur nicknamed "Mr. Clean" after he shaved his head. Neil Hunter, a silver-haired Australian, had sold his home to buy a boat and enter the race. Another Russian, Viktor Yazykov, had dreamed of the race since he was a teen-ager when he read an article about singlehanded sailors in a smuggled Western magazine.

Three professional sailors in nearly identical boats were set to challenge Autissier and Soldini in the Class One sixty-foot boat division. There was Mike Golding, an ex-firefighter from Great Britain, and his countryman, Josh Hall, whose boat sank in the last race after hitting a shipping container in the middle of the Atlantic. The third, Marc Thiercelin, a handsome but shy Frenchman, was a bit of a mystery. He placed second in the 1996 Vendee Globe, but in Charleston he kept a low profile, avoiding the parties and other events. The day before, he missed a press conference the skippers were required to attend. His absence infuriated Soldini, who stormed out of the Maritime Center's conference room, looking angry and betrayed.

"The damn French. He knows we're all supposed to play the game."

heaviest, sturdiest, and most expensive boat in the fleet. He poured more than $1.7 million of his own money into the blue boat. Then the gold market went south. A week before the start, he was broke. To keep his campaign alive, he sold T-shirts, and for ten to twenty dollars, he put names on his boat's hull. More than 400 people people paid to send their names around the world.

Nearby, Neal Petersen smiled and spoke with friends in his singsong South African accent. A skinny man with tousled

At 8:30 a.m., Davie still hadn't worked out his problems. He told race officials that he might miss the start. Two other skippers also were having trouble. Neil Hunter was still tuning a new rig. Two weeks before, a storm had swept through Charleston and snapped off his mast while he was repairing a shroud. It had been a mad scramble to find a new mast in time, and he still had work to do. Viktor Yazykov had arrived in Charleston only three days before and also needed more time for repairs.

At 9:00 a.m., tow boats pulled out the first yachts. Several hundred onlookers jammed the Maritime Center's piers, cheering and waving with each departure. First off the docks was Petersen, standing on his tiny red yacht, *www.no-barriers.com*, named after his Internet site. One by one, the yachts were towed past the city's Waterfront Park with its large pineapple fountain, and then by The Battery with its handsome old mansions. Standing on the bow of his candy-apple red yacht, *Cray Valley*, J.P. Mouligne shadowboxed in the direction of Mike Garside, an ex-boxer. Two months before, the two dueled in a race to Charleston. They had nearly identical boats, but Mouligne whipped Garside by twenty-one hours. Both were keen on another round.

As the parade moved past Fort Sumter toward the rock jetties protecting the mouth of Charleston Harbor, the breeze began to build - and so did the number of spectator boats. They poured out from the city's inlets, streams and marinas. Pontoon boats, trimarans, catamarans, ketches, sloops, johnboats, schooners, tug boats and Jet Skis. One sailboat sported a banner: "Godspeed Guys." By 11:00 a.m., it was a giant floating party, and the harbor was a forest of masts and sails. Thin clouds gave the sky a silvery tint. Forty Coast Guard and police boats tried to keep boaters from running into each other. Indeed, the start can be as dangerous as any hurricane. In the 1986-87 race, two racers collided, and joyriders in a stolen

spectator boat got snagged in another skipper's lines, causing the spectator boat to capsize.

Five-hundred-strong, the spectator fleet converged on a place ironically called the safety zone: a boxed-shaped area just beyond the jetties set aside only for the racers. Two Coast Guard vessels marked the starting line. The winds continued to pick up. Outside the safety zone, the scene began to look like a giant bumper boat ride. The swells grew to about five feet, and passengers in the smaller spectator boats bounced around as if they were riding mechanical bulls. When the cabin cruiser pulling Mouligne's yacht released its line, heavy swells knocked the tow boat on its side three times, breaking tables and lamps inside the boat.

By 11:30 a.m., the juices inside Mark Schrader's stomach

INTO THE WIND

were raging. Schrader was the race director. From his perch aboard the 210-foot Coast Guard cutter *Diligence*, he watched the tow boats fight a swift incoming tide. Several yachts hadn't made it to the safety zone.

Soldini radioed Schrader and suggested delaying the noon start.

"We're trying to do it on time for a whole bunch of reasons," Schrader radioed back.

But fifteen minutes before noon, Schrader announced that the race would be postponed until 12:15 p.m.

Then a cannon went off.

"What the hell was that?" Schrader said.

"They decided to have a signal for the postponement," someone answered.

Schrader rolled his eyes and took a deep breath. Fearing that the skippers may have thought the race had begun, he and other officials frantically radioed each boat, advising them of the delay and urging them to remove any crew members from their yachts.

"*Balance Bar* has been plucked," Schrader shouted into his radio at 12:06 p.m., referring to crew members leaving Brad Van Liew's boat.

"*Modern U.* has been plucked," Schrader said six minutes later.

In the safety zone, Neal Petersen sailed along the line, while Soldini, Thiercelin and Hall tacked to gain an advantage. Isabelle Autissier hung back. She did this whenever she started a long race. Wary of collisions, she knew that crossing the line first didn't matter much in a 27,000-mile race.

"All clear, crews are all clear. Everyone is sailing solo," Schrader said at 12:13 p.m.

"Here we go folks."

At 12:15 p.m., Shelly Pullen, a sixth-grader from a local middle school, fired an old brass Coast Guard cannon.

Petersen was first over the line, but then the speedy sixty-footers took over, passing him within seconds. Josh Hall

cranked up his stereo, and The Doors blared from his cockpit, as his bright green and yellow boat heeled in the wind. The bigger boats picked up speed, matching the Coast Guard cutter's eleven-knot pace. At 12:44 p.m., Robin Davie surprised race officials by making it across the starting line.

The fleet glided toward the horizon, southeast toward the Gulf Stream and several tropical storms churning in the Atlantic. Suddenly the boats looked smaller and the ocean larger, an endless prairie of green and white.

J.P. Mouligne on *Cray Valley*

Joshua Slocum & Adventure Inc.

An hour after the start, J.P. Mouligne suddenly felt like crying. The whole thing was too much to take in. He had spent more than eight years planning for this race, finding a sponsor, building a boat, lining up a top-notch shore crew. Then, in Charleston, there were press conferences and parties and people asking him to sign their Around Alone posters and shirts. More than 150 people from France and the United States flew in to see him off. He felt like an actor starring in a sailing drama. It was a fantasy world, show business. Just like the old days when he was throwing knives.

Now, he was on the water, watching his bright red yacht, *Cray Valley,* dance through the waves. Finally, he could be himself.

A handsome, square-jawed man, Mouligne was a little surprised at how much the post-start letdown affected his emotions. He was no stranger to the spotlight. Mouligne grew up in a mansion outside Paris. His father, a former pilot for Air France and French cotton tycoon Marcel Boussac, hoped his son would follow him into the skies. But Mouligne was a listless, unfocused teen-ager. His frustrated parents eventually sent him to a school in downtown Paris. There he met a philosophy teacher who told him he could be anything he wanted to be. Mouligne decided to become a juggler.

He performed on street corners and cabarets in the city's red light district. Soon, he graduated to knives, learning how to toss them in an imaginary box half an inch wide by one and a half inches long, accurate enough to zing them at his brother. As will happen, his girlfriend took his brother's place in the act, and the two traveled across Europe and Africa under the stage name *Duo Taranis* (the God of Thunder Pair). He was on television several times, and as the act's popularity grew, so did the pressure to do more dangerous stunts. He started tossing fourteen-inch knives blindfolded. Then one night in Italy, he was a little off, and a knife hit his partner's finger. He started having confidence problems. A nervous knife thrower is a dangerous knife thrower. One night in Zimbabwe, he handed his blades out to the audience and quit.

The market for a retired knife thrower without a college degree was limited, so he flew to America, landing a job with his brother, Patrick, who owned a fiberglass company in Rhode Island. He became a salesman, sometimes winning over clients with an impromptu knife-tossing demonstration. He bought and moved aboard a Nantucket 33. In his spare time, he entered sailing races.

His knife-throwing years prepared him well for offshore sailing competitions. He had an uncanny ability to stay cool and

Duo TARANIS

focused under pressure. Over time, he compiled a solid racing resume. He befriended Isabelle Autissier, studied how methodically she worked on deck, how intent she was in trying to understand the ocean's winds and rhythms, how hard she pushed her boat.

Now, here he was in one of the most difficult sailing races ever conceived, competing against his mentor. His dream had come true. It was wonderful and overwhelming. He was emotionally spent. Tears welled in his eyes. He sat in his cabin for a few moments, soaking it in. Alone. At last.

Two days later, Mouligne was in his cabin when the phone rang.

"May I speak to J.P. please?" the ComSat operator said.

Mouligne chuckled. Who else would answer the phone?

Mouligne and the other skippers would soon realize that the ocean is not a lonely place. That morning, as Mouligne talked on the satellite phone, he also typed an e-mail that he would send via satellite, which would be zapped to the Internet and be read by thousands of sailing fans. While he tapped away on his laptop's keyboard, the autopilot steered the boat, and a satellite global positioning system updated his location every few minutes. Above his chart table, a single-sideband radio could be used to contact other skippers, other boats, or a marine telephone operator. He also had a VHF radio for short-range communication. A desalinator, meanwhile, made some fresh water.

"The technology we use on board is unbelievable," he said in an e-mail to the Race Operations Center that day.

The ROC (pronounced Rock) was in an unremarkable one-story office building in downtown Charleston, a five-minute walk from the docks. Race officials manned the banks of computers, radios and other communications equipment twenty-four hours a day, seven days a week. The race's primary sponsor was ComSat Mobile Communications, a company based in

Maryland that operated a global satellite communications network. Using ComSat's equipment and expertise, race coordinators bounced satellite signals to the boats with a few taps on their keyboards. From their boats, the skippers did the same. These signals might contain e-mail messages, reports on weather conditions, digital photos, even video recordings. Every six hours, the ROC electronically polled the fleet to monitor its progress, and then sent the boats' positions to the race's Internet Web site, www.aroundalone.com. This marriage of satellite and Internet technology made the race a spectator sport. By logging onto the race's Web site, armchair sailors could track skippers' courses, read their e-mails, find out what they had for dinner, or whether they missed their girlfriends. On a typical day, 5,000 to 10,000 people visited the Web site, more when trouble happened.

It was a far different world on April 24, 1895, when a wiry American named Joshua Slocum slipped out of Boston Harbor in his 37-foot sloop *Spray*. Slocum spent the next three years at sea, surviving run-ins with pirates, food poisoning and violent storms. He became the first person to sail alone around the world, and his book, *Sailing Alone Around the World*, inspired generations of sailors to look toward the sea for solitude and adventure. However, it would be another seventy years before long-distance singlehanded sailing really took off. In the mid-1960s, British sailor Francis Chichester sailed around the world in his ketch, *Gipsy Moth IV*. His circumnavigation captured the world's imagination and, in 1968, prompted England's *Sunday Times Golden Globe* newspaper to sponsor the first nonstop singlehanded race around the world. Nine men started. One committed suicide along the way. Another decided near the end that he didn't want the fame that would come with winning and steered toward Tahiti. Only British skipper Robin Knox Johnston finished. It took him 312 days.

Another fourteen years would pass before the next solo race

around the world. In 1982, after a regatta in Newport, Rhode Island, several sailors dreamed up an idea over a few beers to do a round-the-world race from America. While looking for sponsors, they bumped into Nigel Rowe, chief executive of corporate relations with The BOC Group, a large multinational corporation based in Britain. Rowe, a sailing enthusiast, convinced his company to pay the race's bills, and The BOC Challenge was born. Under the guidance of race director Robin Knox Johnston, a quirky collection of adventurers left Newport that year, including a Czechoslovakian mariner who sought political asylum just before the start and a Japanese Zen Buddhist taxi driver who played the saxophone (and would commit suicide during the 1990-91 race after a poor showing in the second leg.)

While the BOC fleet raced around the globe, Mark Schrader was doing his own solo circumnavigation, raising money for a school for emotionally disabled children near his home in the Seattle area. During his voyage, he kept on bumping into the BOC skippers. He liked these characters and the fraternal feelings the race created and decided to give it a shot in 1986. He finished in 175 days. Schrader was an athletic man with a medium build and a thick salt-and-pepper beard. He grew up on a farm in Nebraska and rode a horse to his one-room school. He never saw the ocean until he was a teen-ager. But by the age of forty, he had twice navigated the world's most dangerous and remote oceans. In 1990, The BOC Group asked him to be race director.

In 1994, organizers moved the race from Newport to Charleston, feeling that the Rhode Island sailing community wasn't behind the event. The move was a gamble. Newport was America's most prominent yachting community, while Charleston had just a handful of marinas and yacht businesses. Still, the city had a fine natural harbor. The College of Charleston had one the nation's best collegiate sailing teams. City leaders were enthusiastic. Indeed, the city welcomed the event with a mixture of puzzlement and faith, not really know-

Joshua Slocum on *Spray*

Mark Schrader

ing what it was about. Volunteers stepped forward to house the skippers in the city's well-preserved antebellum neighborhoods. Local boaters exhausted everyone with a battery of parties and festivals. After the race, New York City boaters tried to lure the event north, but Schrader and other race officials chose to stick with Charleston as the host port in 1998. When The BOC Group decided in 1995 not to sponsor the event, organizers changed the name to Around Alone. In addition to Charleston, the fifth edition would stop in Cape Town, South Africa, Auckland, New Zealand, and Punta del Este, Uruguay, before returning to Charleston eight months later.

During busy times in the race, Schrader often seemed lost in thought, as if juggling too many balls. He was easily frustrated by people who got in his way, furrowing his brow when people didn't live up to promises. His style was like a college basketball coach. He barked orders to skippers and their crews and anyone else in his way. Some skippers bristled under his authoritarian style, but they also knew he was a fiercely loyal man who loved sailing and had a deep respect for everyone who made it to the starting line. Schrader had little patience for critics. He could yell at his team, but if anyone else did, he would chew their heads off.

Schrader's alter ego was Dan McConnell, who handled the marketing and press for the race. A burly man with a warm handshake, McConnell seemed imperturbable around even the most arrogant and aggressive media people. "Mark and I are opposites, and that's why we blend together so well," he said a few days before the start. "When he thinks it's black and white, I'm thinking about grays. He tells me when I'm being too easy, and I tell him when he's being too hard."

Over the years, McConnell had managed more than 150 polar and Himalayan expeditions, sailing campaigns and other high endurance competitions. He began in the early 1980s with the "Million Dollar Fish," a fundraiser for a children's hospital in Seattle. He cooked up an idea to release a tagged salmon in Puget Sound. If someone reeled it in within twenty-

four hours, he or she would net one million dollars. Fourteen thousand boats went after the fish, which escaped the armada. The promotion made national headlines, and McConnell's phone began to ring off the hook. People from all over the world called, saying they were climbing Mount Everest, walking to the North Pole, or sailing around the world, and could he find them a sponsor? One of these people was Mark Schrader, who asked McConnell to help publicize his first solo circumnavigation. McConnell agreed, and also did public relations for Schrader's BOC Challenge race in 1986.

McConnell was intrigued by Schrader and these other adventurers. "Every sailor, every mountain climber has been asked the same question: Why do you do this?" McConnell said. "And no matter what words come out of their mouths, the real answer is, 'I do it for me.' These extreme adventurous pursuits are basically selfish endeavors. In some cases, it is indeed the journey that drives them, not the end of the trail. For others, it's a matter of stepping off the treadmill of daily life, or leaving convention and finding serenity of the soul in nature. These people are thinkers, not just athletes participating in a sport until their abilities fade." McConnell soon found himself promoting these adventurers, following them up glaciers (once he made it to 22,000 feet on Mount Everest) or on a snowmobile tracking the Iditarod in Alaska. He was on a first-name basis with Sir Edmund Hillary, Reinhold Messner and other famous mountain climbers. As the years passed, these extreme sportsmen eventually went mainstream, their adventures chronicled on ESPN, in *USA Today,* and other popular news and entertainment media. It was a trend McConnell watched with a mixture of satisfaction and concern.

While the coverage made it easier for adventurers to find corporations to bankroll their climbs and voyages, legions of new companies sprang up, ready to take people down jungle rapids or into the world's highest mountains for a fee. "In the late 1980s, it was almost impossible to get to Antarctica," McConnell said. "Now, you can pay $45,000 and get on a plane, look at the penguins and leave." He remembers an expedition to Mount Everest he managed in the early 1980s, the first one to originate in China. "Lhasa (in Tibet) was truly a Shangri-La then." Then came an avalanche of adventure tours to the Himalayas. "The next time I went, there was a Holiday Inn with oxygen machines in the rooms. You could sit there sucking on oxygen and watch cable. I don't like that." One day his wife, Jane, cut out a cartoon of a bus on the top of Mount Everest, posing the question "Why climb Mount Everest?" and answering, "Because the bus came here."

The Everest debacle of 1996 made McConnell even more wary. That year, several expeditions ran into trouble, including one led by McConnell's friend, Scott Fischer. Fischer and several others died, their story documented in the bestseller *Into Thin Air*. Critics charged that tour organizers were selling or promoting adventures to people unprepared for the rigors.

The Around Alone and other singlehanded races had seen their share of criticism as well. Technically, singlehanded races violate international maritime regulations, which call for a twenty-four-hour watch, a rule that would be physically impossible for an Around Alone competitor to follow. Instead of a human lookout, solo sailors depend on autopilots to steer their boats while they sleep, cook or make repairs. Radar alarms let them know if they are on a collision course with another vessel. Some pundits and boaters have questioned whether the technology is dependable enough. Others charge that the pressure of competition, fueled by corporate sponsorship, forces skippers to build dangerous boats and push them harder than they should. In 1995, a member of the Olympic Committee told French reporters: "Stop this solo madness." He said the skippers were victims of their sponsors, media and race organizers. Isabelle Autissier promptly responded in the French magazine *Bateau*: "You ought not to treat sportswomen and men like children. Prohibition will not prevent accidents from happening. Solo racing is a great way to develop individual responsibility for ourselves and grow respect for nature, which

we have to preserve. We don't do it for money, glory or to be on television. We all enjoy this deep sensation of total human freedom and responsibility. And we will surely continue."

Still, solo sailing races, no matter how you looked at them, were risky business. In the history of the three singlehanded circumnavigation races - the 1968 Golden Globe, the Around Alone, the Vendee Globe - five out of 127 skippers, or 3.9 percent, were lost at sea, a higher fatality rate than the 3.3 percent who die every year trying to scale Mount Everest. Never had an entire fleet made it back in one piece. The attrition rate ranged from thirty to almost ninety percent.

Throughout their association and friendship, Schrader and McConnell constantly wrestled with the responsibilities of running a safe race and their desire to maintain the event's spirit of independence and adventure. They went through an especially intense period of soul-searching after the 1994-95 race. While heading toward Cape Horn, British skipper Harry Mitchell disappeared. A spry 72-year-old with a keen sense of humor and a penchant for taking off his clothes at pool parties, Mitchell was extremely well-liked in singlehanded sailing circles. His death hit both of them hard, especially Schrader. He and Mitchell had sailed in the 1986-87 race, and his friend died under his watch. Schrader vowed that the 1998-99 race would be the safest ever. New race rules required that boats have special watertight bulkheads so the boats wouldn't sink. Each boat would have a motor with a propeller in case of an emergency. He made sure the boats had the best communications and search-and-rescue devices available. Coast Guard officers in Washington, D.C., took notice and said the safety features were among the best they had ever seen for a sailing race. In the event's defense, Schrader often was quoted as saying that, per mile, sailing in the Around Alone was a safer bet than driving. Nevertheless, despite all the precautions, he knew anything could happen. Like a father watching his sons and daughters go on their first dates, he would be a nervous wreck for most of the race.

Dan McConnell

Atlantic
Ocean

Lesser
Antilles

Venezuela

Tropical Storm Lisa
GOES-8 4KM Resolution
Channel 4 Enhanced IR
October 6, 1998 1415 UTC

NOAA

A Storm Named Lisa

CHAPTER FOUR

T hwap.

Isabelle Autissier saw it at the last second, too late to take evasive action. A flying fish streaked across her boat like a cruise missile and slammed into her right eye, giving her a big fat shiner.

"I would like to protest," she joked in an e-mail to the ROC six days after the start. The attack "is strictly forbidden by race rules."

Other than getting smacked in the face by a fish, her first week at sea had been rather uneventful. One day she drifted for three windless hours. At first it bothered her, these calms. But the water's beauty touched her heart. At certain times of the day, the sea was a dark violet, as smooth as a pane of glass, and the clouds were like giant cotton balls. She, like most of the other skippers in the race, sailed naked. Why not? No one was around, and the heat often was unbearable, especially when winds were light. She was concerned about dehydration and monitored her body for the first signs - a headache or unusual fatigue. She drank as much as three gallons of water a day. During the afternoons, she took refuge in the shade of the mainsail, watching the wind, then dashing over to the autopilot to correct her course. It was so hot that she could only stay on deck for thirty minutes before ducking into the cabin.

As the sun set, it was more pleasant outside, and one windless night, she put some classical music on the stereo, a piece featuring the cello. When she sailed alone, she felt everything more deeply, her emotions, her thoughts. The gentle, mournful music seemed to mirror the spirit of the calm seas and humid, heavy air. Perfect, she thought.

The first leg from Charleston to Cape Town, South Africa, was the longest - about 7,000 miles. The dangers were fewer than the swirling winds below Africa and South America, but this stretch would test the skippers' sailing and forecasting skills. The trick was to find the quickest route to and through the doldrums, a windless band near the equator. The best route wasn't always a straight line. Sometimes skippers sailed far off course, looking for winds that might take them south faster. Autissier had done this in 1994, heading farther east than the rest of the fleet. She found the right winds and arrived in Cape Town five days ahead of her nearest rival.

In this race, Giovanni Soldini made a similar gamble, taking a northeasterly route. "People were saying, 'Hey Giovanni, there's not a buoy in Gibraltar,'" he recalled later. "I was laughing because I was sure it was the right way." Soon, he realized

the joke was on him.

Early October is the heart of hurricane season, and the route south was like sailing through a shooting gallery. Hot winds blew off the African continent, twirling into tropical depressions in the warm equatorial waters of the Atlantic. As Soldini and the others made their way through the Sargasso Sea, a tropical storm began to spin fast enough to earn a name, Lisa. Soldini and the rest of the front-runners settled down to their chart tables and tried to find a way to use Lisa's winds as a slingshot toward the doldrums. The more he looked at the storm's forecast, the less he liked it. Lisa was changing direction and growing stronger. Soldini suddenly realized he would be in the wrong position. The energy of the storm would create a vacuum behind it, leaving him bobbing in an area with no winds. He cursed his bad luck.

"I don't have wind, so I'm not happy," he said in an e-mail to the ROC. "That is the life." Three days later, he wrote another. "Hi there. Here, as usual, there's virtually no wind. I really can't believe it. It's the fifth or sixth consecutive day like this. What's worse is that it looks like the others are roaring along at 10 knots .... Patience. Ciao, Giovanni."

Taking bold but calculated risks was part of Soldini's nature and typical of some of the world's best singlehanded sailors. Even as a young boy, Soldini had a powerful independent streak. "We nicknamed him *La Bestia* (The Beast)," said his father, Adolfo. "Gio was extremely lively and wishing to do things even at eleven months. He was neither obedient nor rebellious, but extremely independent. If you convinced him to do something, he would do it to the end. If you didn't, no way. If he participated in a competition, he pretended to win." Soldini wasn't much of a student and at sixteen failed to graduate to the next grade level. "I remember him saying, 'I will not repeat the class. It is too boring. I will find a way to go sailing to the Caribbean and come back in time to prepare my exams privately,'" his father recalled.

Soldini went to Palma, Mallorca, a Mediterranean island off the coast of Spain where many European boats tarry before they cross to the Caribbean in the winter. He found a job on one and made his first transatlantic crossing. On his way back, he found work on an old thirty-seven-footer whose captain had polio and had little use of his legs. The only other crew member had never sailed in his life. During the crossing, the tiny boat ran into some rough weather, and Soldini wrote in his journal how the waves were like the Italian Alps, and that the clear mountain air was similar to rainwashed air after a squall. He loved cruising to new places and meeting people from different cultures. With his disarming laugh and easygoing manner, he made friends easily. But his carefree personality masked an intense yearning to compete.

His first successful race was in 1991 when he placed third in the Baule-Dakar race. In the 1992 Europe One Star, he was leading his class when he struck a chunk of ice. The collision

Mike Golding on *Team Group 4*

wrecked his rudder and put a hole in the hull. Soldini repaired the leak, and using a spinnaker pole as a spare rudder, managed to place second in the fifty-foot boat class. In his next race, from Quebec to France, the boat lost its keel and capsized. Soldini and his crew were in the cockpit and dove into the cabin to retrieve the survival gear. They were rescued fourteen hours later. Since 1992, he had won five major sailing races and finished second in the 1994-95 BOC Challenge. His fame in Italy soared. "Sometimes," he said, "when I walk down the street in Milan, people say 'Hey, Giovanni,' and sometimes it's very nice. But I don't like being a celebrity too much because then your job becomes being a celebrity, and you don't go sailing as much."

While Soldini struggled through calms, British skipper Mike Golding aimed for the center of Hurricane Lisa. He spent hours drawing sketches with times and speeds, trying to figure out a plan.

Fellow Brit Josh Hall was thirty miles ahead of Golding and watched his rival close in on the eye with growing apprehension. Doesn't he know he's on a collision course with a hurricane? Hall raised Golding on the radio.

"I think you're sailing into danger," he said.

"I don't think it's that well-developed," Golding radioed back.

Hall had a satellite image of the storm on his computer, and he shook his head. It showed a very well-formed hurricane.

Soon, Golding was about fifteen miles from the eye in 45-mph winds. That was close enough, he thought, turning south-

west to steer clear. As he sailed away, he could see the bolts of lightning dancing around the eye wall.

Hall caught the southern tail of the hurricane's winds and screamed south. One afternoon he was on the deck steering and looked at the speed gauge - twenty-eight knots and holding steady. It was an exhilarating feeling, going this fast using only the wind. His boat, like Soldini's and Autissier's, was designed by Groupe Finot. It was regarded as the fastest and lightest of the new sixty-footers, though it had a decidedly slow name, *Gartmore Investment Management*, the name of his sponsor. When the boat reached high speeds, the rudder hummed at a high pitch. Down below, waves pounded the carbon-fiber hull, sounding like cannonball strikes. Every now and then a two-foot wall of water blasted across the deck. The sound of rushing water was everywhere.

Something caught his eye, and he looked to the right. There, about four yards away, was a flying fish streaking along in a parallel course to the boat, as if in a race. Slowly, Hall's boat began to pull ahead. He looked at the speed gauge. Still twenty-eight knots. He smiled. He had always wanted to know how fast a flying fish flew.

Hall was having a much better race than the last go around. In the 1994-95 BOC Challenge, his yacht slammed into what he suspects was a partially submerged shipping container. The boat began to sink, and he phoned the ROC, which immediately diverted another skipper, Alan Nebauer, to his position - about twelve hours away. Using pumps, Hall managed to stay afloat. Nebauer arrived just in time. Hall grabbed his laptop computer, jumped into his life raft, and watched his yacht go under.

Four years later, he had a new and better boat, complete with two computers and a thunderous DVD movie player and sound system. So far, it had been a problem-free voyage. But as dusk fell on October 6, in choppy warm waters churned up by Hurricane Lisa, he spotted trouble on his forestay. The roller-furling gear was coming apart, preventing him from using one of his most powerful sails. He would have to climb the mast. This was no night job. So he waited until the next morning to do the repair. When dawn broke, he turned the boat so it would run downwind. Using a bosun's chair, which resembles the seat on a child's swing, he slowly raised himself up the mast. The winds blew at a steady 20 mph, and the boat pitched in the eight-foot seas. About halfway up, he used another line to swing to the forestay. Clinging like a squirrel to a power line, Hall spent four hours sorting out the situation. Suddenly the boat jibed, trapping a halyard he needed to lower himself to the deck. Stuck in midair, he watched his boat crash through the waters below. "What the hell am I doing?" he said to himself. He climbed out of the bosun's chair and shimmied down the forestay like a nervous cat.

Lisa reshuffled the deck. The shy French skipper of *SOMEWHERE*, Marc Thiercelin, and Isabelle Autissier found themselves with the best winds heading into the doldrums. But Autissier's good luck didn't last. On October 5, she was eating breakfast when she heard a bang in the front of the boat. It was a bad, unnatural sound. She looked forward. The forestay had snapped at a solid stainless steel fitting near the bow. That's trouble, she thought. Like a guy wire holding up a radio tower, the forestay helps keep up the mast. Without the forestay, a sudden squall could knock it down. She watched the mast move back and forth about six feet. No time to waste. She used a rope to tie the loose line, slowing the mast's movement. She went below and phoned her shore crew for advice. They exchanged e-mails, and Autissier decided to use a halyard as a replacement. She waited for the wind to die and tied on the halyard, trying to get the tension right. She worked for four hours. It was tough going, and her arms soon were covered with bruises. Eventually, she felt the tension was correct.

Marc Thiercelin

But she knew she couldn't fly her big genoa sail, which put her at a competitive disadvantage. She sent a message to race headquarters: "At the moment, the rhythm is very irregular: one day slaving away, the next all is well. But the life of a singlehanded sailor is always a little like that. The secret is to rest when you have the chance. All in all, I am pretty much on track."

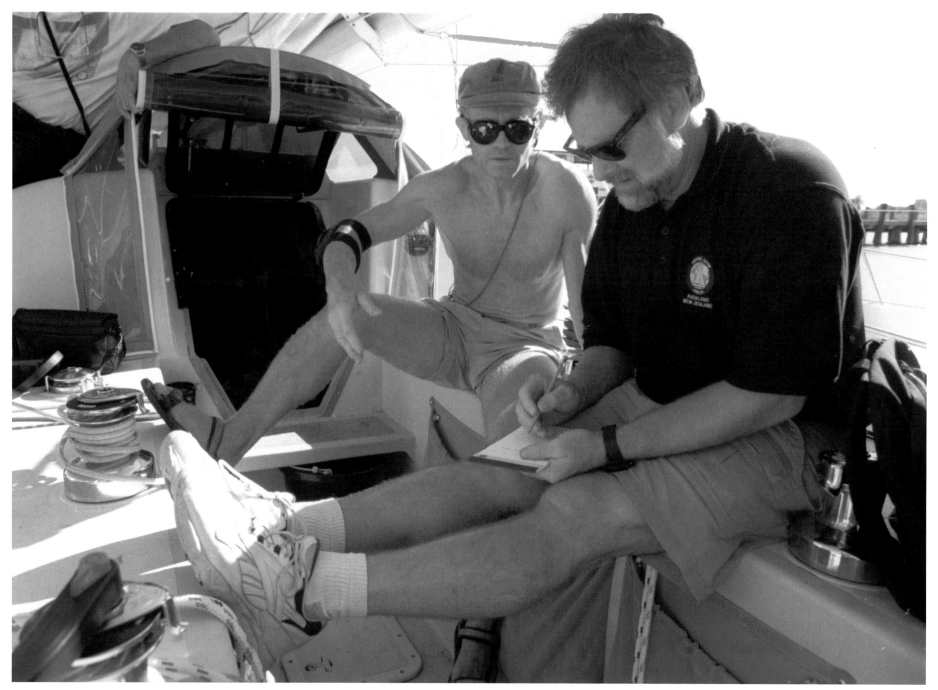

Viktor Yazykov and Mark Schrader

The Clouds Hang Heavy

On October 1, five days after the start, Viktor Yazykov was still at the dock in Charleston. It was a warm afternoon, and the sinking sun gave the harbor a golden tint. Yazykov stood shirtless on his yacht, *Wind of Change-Russia,* with elbow braces on both arms. At fifty, he still had a body-builder's physique and a boyish face with blond hair, blue eyes, and a smile that revealed a gold tooth. He was waiting for Mark Schrader to check his boat and ask him questions for the race's insurance policy. Then, finally, he could leave.

Yazykov had arrived in Charleston just three days before the start after a long transatlantic crossing from his home in Sochi, a small fishing village on the Black Sea. But his journey really began in 1964 when he was sixteen. Yazykov managed to get his hands on a banned Western sailing magazine. In it, an article told of solo sailors traveling to exotic places. The adventure appealed to the small-town boy, and so did the lives of freedom these sailors led. Although his father, a fisherman, had drowned just two years before, Yazykov felt no bitterness toward the sea. He learned to sail, taking out boats whenever he could. He learned to tie knots and do repairs with both hands, knowing these skills might come in handy if he were out in the ocean alone. He did pull-ups on a metal bar to strengthen his mast-climbing muscles. He swam in cold water so sailing in

frigid seas wouldn't be a shock. He practiced exercises to prevent sea sickness: breathe ... close your eyes ... move your head in one direction ... breathe ... move your head in another direction ... breathe. Eventually he ended up at a Soviet nautical college and then in the Soviet Army. He fought in Afghanistan. He was a paratrooper, and when the Chernobyl nuclear reactor melted down, the army sent him into the area to help with the cleanup. The radiation made him sick. Through all this, he kept dreaming of the sea. Some day he would sail around the world.

Standing on the docks in Charleston that afternoon, he looked relaxed and in no real hurry to get moving. He smiled and told a friend, "I spend my life to get to this point."

When Schrader and the other race officials arrived, they climbed onto Yazykov's yacht and went below. They tested his communications system. Schrader placed a seal on the motor, which was to be used only in emergencies. If the seal was broken, the skipper would be disqualified. With the seal in place, Schrader and Yazykov sat in the cockpit. "I have to ask you some questions about your sailing experience. The insurance company needs this," Schrader said. Yazykov nodded. "OK, no problem."

Yazykov said he worked with the Soviet fishing fleet in the North Pacific. Later he joined the team that built *Fazisi,* the So-

INTO THE WIND

viet entry in the 1989-90 Whitbread race. He told of how he returned to Sochi after the Whitbread and built his own thirty-foot boat, dragging chestnut trees from the forest for materials. He entered the 1992 Europe One Star, a transatlantic race from Plymouth, England, to Newport, Rhode Island. After the race, he and an American, Bob Adams, spent six years planning for the Around Alone. They built identical yachts, *Wind of Change-Russia* and *Wind of Change-America.* Yazykov listed other races. "That's enough," Schrader said with a smile. "Sail safe. You've worked hard for this."

Moments later, a tow boat pulled him into the harbor, and as the sun set over the city's skyline, Yazykov hoisted his sails.

So sad.

As Yazykov sailed into the Atlantic, a wave of emptiness engulfed him. It had been so much work to get here. So many plans and hopes. He and Bob Adams had worked all these years together, built two beautiful boats, but the stress and strain of finishing the project were too much on their friendship. By September they weren't speaking to each other. At the last minute, Adams pulled out of the race when he realized he wouldn't be able to start on time. But Yazykov was determined to join the fleet, no matter what. If only he had more time, he thought. He knew how important it was to be prepared. For years, he had read everything about the race he could get his hands on. He knew that poorly prepared boats didn't stand much of a chance. On the way to Charleston, he was still installing parts.

Wind of Change had sailed beautifully, however. He was so proud of his boat. Sometimes he talked to it. "Please steer properly," he would say. "Stay strong," he would tell the mast and boom. With its sleek lines and twin dagger boards, it looked like a miniature version of the sixty-footers sailed by Isabelle Autissier and Giovanni Soldini. A few puffs of wind and the boat would be trotting along at ten knots.

But now that he was living his dream, everything seemed wrong. He spilled some boiling water on himself. He broke a tooth. The autopilot failed. It was too much. He gave up and let the boat steer itself. Day after day, his mood darkened, even as his yacht caught up to the slower boats. "Take care of me, little boat," he pleaded. He couldn't shake the sadness.

One day, he opened a package of dehydrated food, one of several that another skipper, Brad Van Liew, had given him. Inside the package was a little pouch. Must be the spices, he thought, just like in those cheap noodles we have in Russia. He heated some water and poured it into the foil package. He broke up the smaller pouch and poured the contents in with the dehydrated food.

Another wave of sadness washed over him. He found himself sobbing uncontrollably. He was afraid to go on deck. He stopped eating.

He didn't realize until a few weeks later that the little packets with his dehydrated food weren't spices. They contained a silty gray substance that absorbed moisture. "Do not eat" was written in small red letters on the package in English, French, Spanish and Japanese, but not Russian. Above the warning was a tiny picture of someone eating the packet with a red line across it. The chemicals in the packet seemed to alter his brain chemistry. That and the stress of the start made him dangerously depressed.

Crazy ideas kept popping into his head. He knew his life was in jeopardy. He had to talk to someone.

After ten days at sea, he raised a marine operator on his single sideband radio who patched him through to his wife, Ludmila.

"Stay alive," she told him through the static. "You can't leave me now. Viktor, you are a strong man. Please, Viktor, just stay alive."

The sound of his wife's voice caused the clouds in his mind to part.

Everything will be OK now, he told himself after signing off. Everything is OK.

The chemicals in the packet seemed to alter his brain chemistry. That and the stress of the start made him dangerously depressed.

INTO THE WIND

Tough Choices

After three weeks at sea, Isabelle Autissier thought she smelled land. It was a starry night, and her boat *PRB* sailed straight for the eastern bulge of Brazil. She had just crossed the equator, her tenth time in a sailboat. This sunny and humid place was like an old friend. She knew its rhythms, when to fall off and when to add sails. She knew that navigating this often-windless area sometimes was like playing hopscotch. The trick was to find thunderstorms and squalls and hop from one patch of wind to the other.

As she closed in on the coast, she kept a sharp eye out for other boats. The coast of Brazil was a busy one with lots of cargo ships. She also had to watch out for fishermen in *djangadas*, small rafts with lateen rigs. The men would remove the rigs when they started fishing. Standing on the rafts awash in the coastal chop, the fishermen were nearly invisible, especially after dark. To keep awake, she thought about her first transatlantic voyage.

That was eleven years earlier, on her thirty-foot steel boat *Parole*, which means "word" or "communication" in French. For three years, she spent nights and weekends welding the boat. Brazil was her first landfall in the Americas. She was a scientist then, teaching and doing fisheries research in La Rochelle, a coastal city in France's Bay of Biscay. She spent a

year wandering on *Parole*. It was a wonderful adventure. The solitude was good for her soul. When she was alone, emotions felt stronger, colors brighter. Every action and thought seemed to have more meaning. Afterward, she yearned for more time on the water. Later that year, she entered her first solo race, the Mini Transat, which started in France, stopped in the Canary Islands and finished in the Antilles. She had a scientist's approach to ocean races. She studied weather forecasts, satellite photos and charts for hours, looking for secrets amid the isobars. She won the first leg and finished third overall. Within a few years, she would quit her job as a scientist and race full time.

So much had changed, she thought, as her boat sliced through the waves.

After coming within eleven miles of the coast, she steered away from Brazil and her past. She felt good. She had picked a fine route through the fluky winds and heat of the planet's mid-section. She was in the front of the pack and perfectly positioned for the trade winds that would send her flying toward South Africa.

Giovanni Soldini, however, was having a miserable time clawing his way through the doldrums. "You virtually go from storm conditions with 30 knots of wind one minute to five

Sebastian Reidl on *Project Amazon*

knots the next," he complained in an e-mail to the ROC on October 14. "You never get a moment's rest, and the sleepless nights are beginning to tell. My hands are a mess from the saltwater."

Several other skippers also had their hands full. Robin Davie had made it out of Charleston minutes behind the fleet, but *South Carolina* still looked like a floating hardware store as he tried to finish repairs while underway. When he wrapped up one job, something else broke. First the alternator went out, then the ballast pump. "I felt a bit glum about how we could do," Davie told the ROC in an e-mail. "And that wasn't helped the following day when the only electric autopilot went out." To solve the ballast problem, he would flood the bilge and use a small electric bilge pump to fill the ballast tanks. "Alternators - well, we'll just live in nighttime darkness and do without the cassettes, and we'll probably get by," Davie said.

It was even worse on Sebastian Reidl's boat, *Project Amazon*. One week into the race, water seeped into his fuel tank. Suddenly, Reidl had no power to run his communications equipment, stove and autopilot. The entire boat smelled like a diesel tank. The fumes were both annoying and dangerous. Reidl tried to filter the water with toilet paper and paper towels. No luck. Then he discovered some rubbing alcohol and added it to the contaminated fuel. Knowing that alcohol would cause the water and diesel fuel to separate, he carefully si-

phoned off the water. He took the remaining diesel and cranked up the generator. It coughed back to life, but Reidl had only a fraction of the fuel he had before, and he was still 5,000 miles from Cape Town. The final blow came when the boom on his forward rig fell after a halyard block atop the mast broke. Using suction cups, the 59-year-old Canadian climbed the 86-foot-tall mast like Spider-Man but wasn't able to repair the damage.

Reidl was no stranger to challenges. Born in Hungary on the eve of World War II, he fled at the age of five with his mother and two sisters, just ahead of the Russian troops. As a young man, he hitchhiked from Cape Town to Cairo. Later, he moved to Vancouver and formed a mining company in South America. He entered the Around Alone partly to bring attention to the fiery destruction of the Upper Amazon rain forests. He sank his fortune into *Project Amazon*, the most controversial boat in the fleet. While the other sixty-foot boats were made of carbon composites, Reidl's boat had an aluminum hull and a shape that allowed it to ride on a carpet of bubbles, reducing its friction. The boat was heavier, but Reidl figured it would be more durable, especially for the wicked winds of the southern Indian and Pacific oceans. But after the fleet left Charleston, the Europeans in their wide Finot boats left Reidl in their wakes. Despite its innovative design, *Project Amazon* was slow, so slow that some of the smaller and older boats had passed him. This wasn't his race. Reidl went to his computer and sent a message to the ROC.

"I decided that my arrival in Cape Town would be too late to repair my now existing deficiencies and be ready for the next leg of the race," he wrote, formally withdrawing from the competition. He signed off, "One disappointed skipper, Sebastian," and turned west toward Puerto Rico.

At times, it seemed as if Fedor Konioukhov might also end up on some Caribbean shoal. As soon as he left Charleston, he took a more southerly route than the rest of the fleet. The move baffled race officials because his course took him to an area that traditionally has light winds. Konioukhov didn't speak much English. He also didn't check in with the ROC like the other skippers, so organizers were left to track his position and shrug their shoulders.

What they didn't know was that Konioukhov was struggling without a working water ballast system. Ballast helps a boat maintain its stability and course, and without it, Konioukhov found himself pushed south and west by the prevailing winds, right into a windless hole.

Indeed, like Robin Davie and Viktor Yazykov, Konioukhov had a rough ride to the starting line. In early September, while sailing to Charleston, he ran into Hurricane Danielle, 600 miles off the Southeast U.S. coast. High winds pounded his yacht, pinning it on its side for three days. Water poured in and filled the cabin. Worried that the boat would break apart, he launched his life raft. Then, he watched in amazement as a gust lifted the raft into the sky like a kite. A line holding the life raft to the boat snapped, and it flew away. Of all the mountain climbs and trekking adventures he had experienced, this lousy trip to Charleston scared him the most. He expected to drown, but the winds eventually died down. The storm pushed him toward land, and a Coast Guard team towed his battered boat into Charleston. The whole experience set him back weeks. He tried to do as many repairs as possible before the start but wasn't able to fix the ballast system in time.

During the entire month of October, Konioukhov drifted south before hitting any strong winds. Then, off the coast of Brazil, he noticed that some of the screws holding on his keel had come loose. The boat began to take on water, about five buckets per day.

Losing a keel is about the worst thing that can happen to a sailboat. Without the keel, it could quickly capsize. As he watched the water trickle in, he began to fear the worst. "What do I do to survive?" Konioukhov thought. He remembered how a skipper in the last Vendee Globe nearly died after his yacht lost its keel. The skipper lived in an air pocket inside the overturned yacht for four days before being rescued. Konioukhov didn't trust life rafts after watching his fly away in the hurricane. He made up his mind: No matter what, he would stay with the boat. He prepared a special net that he could use as a bed if the boat flipped and went to work on the keel nuts. He tightened them slightly but wasn't sure it did any good. The water continued to seep in.

Race officials grew more and more concerned.

"I suggest you go to Brazil," Mark Schrader said in a message.

If I do that, Konioukhov thought, I won't make it to Cape Town in time.

Race rules required him to be in South Africa one week before the race restart, when the fleet would head for Auckland, New Zealand.

So Konioukhov decided to take a chance on his keel. He hugged the coast of Brazil for five days and monitored the leak. The keel seemed OK. The leak wasn't getting any worse. He steered east, toward Africa.

It was a pleasant tropical evening on October 19 as Brad Van Liew sat down for dinner. His purple yacht *Balance Bar* skimmed through the seas at nine knots. He was off the coast of Brazil now. He had his VHF radio on and the static-filled chatter of fishermen speaking rapid-fire Portuguese mixed with sounds of water rushing past the boat's hull.

Suddenly, an English-speaking man with a raspy voice came on the radio. He was hailing an unnamed boat, identifying its longitude, latitude, heading and speed. "Please respond immediately," the voice said firmly.

Those are my coordinates, Van Liew thought. "This is the

Brad Van Liew on *Balance Bar*

U.S. sailing vessel *Balance Bar*," he told the voice. "Sorry, what's going on?"

"This is a Brazilian Navy warship *Frontin*, and we're off your port bow. You are going through a designated military area. We are doing submarine operations. Turn right to a heading of 230 for one hour to clear the area and maintain your current speed."

"I'm really sorry," Van Liew replied. "I'm in a sailboat and I'll do the best I can."

The voice was not happy and began firing questions at Van Liew. Where are you from? What is your mission? What kind of boat? What color? How many people are on board? What are you carrying? What is your physical description? Van Liew started to sweat.

A few minutes later, another voice hailed Van Liew. This man also spoke English but didn't seem so mad.

"You are going from Charleston to Cape Town?"

"Yes," Van Liew replied.

"Are you in the Around Alone?"

"Yeah."

"What place are you in?"

"I'm in first place in the Class Two division."

"Ok, stand by."

The new voice came back on the radio. "I'm going to move everyone out of your way. Whatever heading you want, take it. We're going to escort you through the area."

Van Liew shook his head and smiled.

"Thank you."

A few minutes later a third voice called Van Liew.

"Do you have five minutes to talk?"

"Sure," Van Liew said. "I've got about twenty more days to talk."

"OK, go to channel 72."

The latest inquiry came from a high ranking officer in the Brazilian Navy and a member of the Rio de Janeiro Yacht Club. He told Van Liew he had a racing boat and helped out when the BOC Challenge stopped in Rio during the first two races. Van Liew filled him in on the race, told him that he was just ahead of J.P. Mouligne, the French knife thrower.

"He's a really bad guy," Van Liew joked. "How about moving your operations in his way?"

The officer laughed and said the Brazilian Navy was rooting for Van Liew now because the French always dominate this event. In the dark, about a mile off, the 314-foot helicopter gun ship steamed with Van Liew, escorting him south.

Unlike some of his rivals, Van Liew was having a grand time.

His fifty-foot boat *Balance Bar* was sailing better than he expected. It was an older boat, built for the 1994-95 race. Alan Nebauer had sailed it under the name of *Newcastle Australia*. Despite its age and older design, *Balance Bar* seemed faster upwind than the two new fifty-foot Finot boats manned by Mike Garside and J.P. Mouligne. "All aboard is just peachy," he told the ROC in one message.

Van Liew is a barrel-chested thirty-year-old from California with close-cropped hair and a gung ho, frat-boy sense of humor. He grew up in California but spent his summers sailing in Newport. While a student at the University of Southern California, he decided to enter the 1990 BOC Challenge. So what if he was only twenty-one. He could do it.

No one with any money stepped forward to pay for his campaign, though. Van Liew set aside his dream. It was a bitter disappointment. He had always gotten what he wanted. "Yeah, I was born with a silver spoon," he would say later. He blocked the race from his mind and channeled his frustration into a career in aviation. He breezed through flight school, and by his late twenties had gained enough experience to fly cargo and passenger planes. He could do loops and other aerobatic maneuvers and landed jobs as a stunt flyer for films and TV. At first he thought he would be an airline pilot but decided that the corporate lifestyle wasn't as glamorous as he imagined. With a friend, he set up a company called Aircraft Management Inc. that managed and leased planes for Hollywood stars and corporate chieftains in Southern California.

But something was missing.

"Yeah, you know what I think it was?" he explained. "This may sound really cheesy, but this race is the only thing in my entire life that I said I was going to do that I didn't do. Here I was, successful, things starting to happen for me. My wife and I were making good money, really kicking ass, enjoying ourselves. I had the keys to thirty airplanes in my top drawer and could go anywhere I wanted to, any time I wanted to and do anything I wanted. But I also was reflecting on a childhood that had gone by. And there was this one thing hanging out there that I was just never able to make happen: the Around Alone. And I hate that. I hate that. There is nothing in my personality I hate more than someone saying, 'You can't do that,' or 'You don't have the money.' Whatever the reason. I just hate being told I can't do something."

He could wait twenty years and save enough money to buy a new sixty-footer. Or he could try again while he was young and hungry. He talked it over with his wife, Meaghan, and they agreed that life was too short and fragile to procrastinate. Van Liew entered the Around Alone not really knowing how and where he would find the money to do a solid, safe and competitive campaign. He and his wife maxed out their credit cards, cashed in their IRAs, borrowed money from friends. They knew it would take about half a million dollars to sail in the race in a competitive, used boat. They bought the old *Newcastle Australia* and renamed it *California Challenge*. By the time they were ready to ship his boat in a truck to Charleston their finances were in shambles. They weren't even sure if they would be able to pay the driver.

Then, during their drive across the country, Van Liew learned that Balance Bar, a company that makes nutritional bars, might sponsor his campaign. By the time he reached Charleston, Van Liew had agreed to change the name of the boat to *Balance Bar*. The company gave him enough money to pay the driver, paint the boat purple like a Balance Bar wrapper and start the race.

It was an unusual sponsorship agreement. Each time he got the Balance Bar name or logo in certain newspapers, television markets or any other visible media, the company sent him a check. The dollar amounts varied depending on the circulation or size of the television market. The bigger the exposure, the better the check. Reporters covering the race, for the most part, had been understanding, mentioning the boat's name when they could.

"I was drinking beers with Mike Golding, and he started chuckling because I was saying 'Balance Bar this' and 'Balance Bar that,' and the reporter started chuckling too. So I said, 'Hey, I know this sounds cheesy but the bottom line is that you don't have anything to write about without competitors, and we rely on these sponsors to put money behind my story, and I know it's a pain in the ass and you all are very guarded about this kind of thing, but I can do a better job for you, if you can do a better job for me.'"

To get more media exposure, Van Liew sent lengthy e-mails from his boat to the Balance Bar Web site and race officials, who posted it on the Around Alone web site. "I'm constantly on the computer, doing as many e-mails as I can muster the strength to do, taking photos, doing phone interviews, usually for about two or three hours a day," he said. "There's no question it would be easier without all the media obligations, but life would be easier if you didn't have to work."

So, after his friendly engagement with the Brazilian Navy, Van Liew dutifully sat down in front of his keyboard and tapped out an account of what happened. He zapped it to the ROC, which posted it on the Web site. A newspaper in Los Angeles wrote a brief story. The check was in the mail.

Viktor Yazykov on *Wind of Change-Russia*

Surgery at Sea

CHAPTER SEVEN

A nasty snap woke Viktor Yazykov in the early morning hours of November 7. He crawled out of his cabin and looked up. A shroud on the port side had parted. Bad news, he thought. A shroud helps hold up the mast, and without the wire, a strong gust could topple the mast. The boat pitched and rolled. White foam from the breaking waves blew in streaks across the water. Forgoing his safety harness, he climbed up the mast. One slip and he would be in the water watching his boat sail off. He used a rope to make a temporary repair and climbed down. This was dangerous, he thought. Better to do everything on a full stomach during daylight.

When the sun came up, he went to work. For six hours he climbed up and down the mast. When he was finished, the rig looked strong, but he was exhausted. He stumbled back into his cabin and collapsed on a seat. He was in top physical condition, but he was too tired to eat or do anything else. He sat motionless for a half hour. He took a deep breath, stood up and went to his laptop.

"This early morning, the low port side diagonal broke," he said in a message to the ROC. "Have spent all day up on the mast. It is better now. Keep reduced sails. Bye, Viktor." He sent the message, crawled into his bunk and fell fast asleep.

He woke up the next morning feeling fine - except for that elbow. He had injured both of them on the way to Charleston before the race, but the right one was in especially bad shape with an angry red bulge. The pain was excruciating. He swallowed a handful of aspirin pills and put some greasy Russian medicine on his arm. The next day, though, a sickly yellow spot appeared on the red bulge and his arm began to get numb. Enough was enough. He opened his laptop and switched it on. "Hello to everybody," he wrote to the ROC. "My right elbow looks pretty bad. So I need a doctor advice what to do. Would you please give me an e-mail I can ask for help. Thank you, Viktor."

More than 5,000 miles away, Dr. Dan Carlin sat in his crimson-colored office in downtown Boston's New England Medical Center, dashing off a couple of e-mails to his patients on boats while waiting for an x-ray from a patient in Africa. Carlin wasn't your typical doctor. He ran WorldClinic, a medical practice that used phones, satellites and the Internet to treat patients across the globe. Among his newest patients were the skippers in the Around Alone. Maps of the world covered his office walls, including a laminated three- by four-foot map de-

Viktor Yazykov

37

Dr. Dan Carlin

voted to the Around Alone with pins marking the skippers' positions.

The phone rang. "Hello, this is Pete Dunning." Dunning was the avuncular coordinator of the ROC. "Viktor Yazykov needs your help."

Carlin had met Yazykov in Charleston before the start. He remembered the Russian's chiseled features and vise-like grip. He liked Yazykov. He seemed to be a humble and polite man, and that surprised him a little considering Yazykov's background. Yazykov had been a member of the Speznaz, the Soviet army's special forces, and had fought in Afghanistan. Carlin knew about the Speznaz. During the war, he was a doctor at an Afghan refugee camp in Pakistan. To his patients, the Speznaz was a dark, fearsome force of killers. How ironic, Carlin thought after meeting Yazykov in Charleston, that a decade later he would be his doctor.

After Dunning told him about Yazykov's elbow, Carlin typed an e-mail to the ROC, which would beam it via ComSat's satellite network to Yazykov's boat. Carlin told Yazykov to take some antibiotics, scrub the wound and build a sling for his elbow.

"Notify us immediately if you develop fever or worsening pain," Carlin wrote and pressed the send key.

The morning of November 10, Yazykov responded: "Sorry, short in power ... Did clean the elbow. It does not seem to be an infection. All the skin is glossy and shiny bump. It is red but some place more whiter. It is like a pillow with some liquid inside of it. It seems is not infected from outside. Sorry." He sent another message a minute later. "Hello guys, this is Viktor again, sorry. I think it is pretty simple. Now I can see a couple little spots with a matter through the skin. I would cut it today. We have about four hours before darkness. So I need a doctor directions how to do it properly. Thank you, Viktor."

Carlin frowned when he read Yazykov's e-mail. He had hoped it was only a superficial infection. But Yazykov's e-mail described an abscess. If it ruptured, the infection could spread. Within a day or two, gangrene could set in. He would likely lose his arm then and maybe die. He looked at his Around Alone map. Yazykov was more than 1,000 miles from Cape Town. That ruled out a helicopter rescue. Surgery was the answer.

With a video camera recording, Viktor Yazykov scrubs his elbow, slices into the abscess, and then puts on a tourniquet.

Carlin put his fingers on his keyboard and began typing instructions. He knew he had to be concise. Yazykov's English was good, but miscommunication could be deadly.

...Paint the area over the abscess with the brown iodine solution included in your medical kit. Use a clean gauze pad to apply the iodine solution ...

... Wash your hands thoroughly with soap and water, use the antiseptic towelettes, then put on a pair of the rubber gloves in your kit ...

... When the iodine dries on your skin, gently feel the abscess to find the part of the abscess that is closest to the surface of the skin ...

... Using the sterile scalpel from your medical kit, make a 2 cm long incision into the abscess through the area that feels closest to the surface ...

Carlin tried to imagine the scene. His patient would have no anesthetic, so he had to reassure him but make him understand the cut might be painful.

...Make your incision rapidly. It will hurt less if you do.

... Pus should flow out of the abscess if you have made your incision in the right spot ... It hurts a great deal when you insert the gauze ... Get it down into the depths of the wound as much as possible.

Carlin typed for forty-five minutes, composing two pages of instructions, and e-mailed them to the ROC.

Yazykov responded seventeen minutes later. "Thank you. I have the doctor's directions and it seems to be clear."

Yazykov always talked to his boat, almost like a lover. "Please take care of me, little boat. You are my baby," he would say. With no autopilot, the boat would have to steer itself through the six-foot seas while he sliced open his elbow. He had to work quickly. The afternoon light was fading. He lashed the tiller with a rope and went below. He took off his shirt and strapped a miner's light on his head. Since the abscess was on the underside of his elbow and difficult to see, he put a mirror the size of a dish on the chart table. He scrubbed, put on some rubber gloves, and painted his elbow with brown iodine. Bent over the table, he took the scalpel and made a quick cut.

The pus and blood gushed out, first on the mirror, blocking the view of his elbow, then onto the chart table and cabin floor. So much blood, Yazykov thought. It ran down his legs and

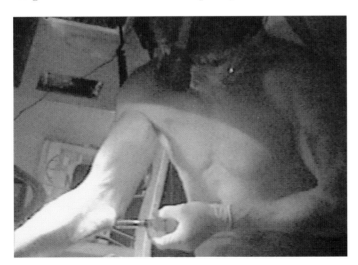

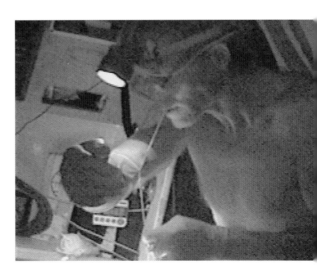

soaked his socks and deck shoes. He tried to stop the bleeding with gauze. No good. The blood began to form a puddle on the floor and splash from side to side as the boat rocked. Yazykov was stunned. He sat on the floor for a half hour, watching the blood drip from his elbow. He didn't know what to do. It was getting dark now. The solar panels wouldn't generate enough electricity to send many messages. He thought: Either I bleed to death or lose the arm. What would a soldier do? He grabbed two bungee cords, and using his teeth and good arm, he tied the cords around his arm seven times to make a tourniquet. It still bled. Soon, his arm felt numb and rubbery. He tried to find a pulse. Nothing. He massaged it and talked to it. "My poor arm. You have worked so hard for me, and I can't save you." He felt weak and ate some chocolate for a quick sugar jolt. He remembered a folk remedy: Red wine helps build blood. Maybe it will help. He found a bottle, uncorked it with his good hand and drank half of it. He stumbled toward the computer. It was 10:00 p.m., and he didn't know if he had enough power to send a message. He typed a message and prayed that he had enough juice.

"Well, this is Viktor. I did it, but it was something unexpected. I could not stop the bleeding. Lost at least half a liter. Placed two shock cords as tight as possible. Bleeding was the same. After bandage it became easier. But now three hours later the hand cannot get the strength back. It feels hot and cold but no strength at all. Please, what should I do before too late? Viktor."

George Fenwick had the night shift at the ROC. When Yazykov's message came in, he grabbed the phone and called Carlin.

"Tell him to remove the shock cords immediately!" Carlin said. Fenwick dashed off a new message relaying Carlin's instructions. Sixteen minutes later, Yazykov sent another short e-mail. "It is not bleeding any more. I took the shock cords off two hours ago, applied hot water massage. It is still cold and weak. Just let me know what else I can do, please." Yazykov

began to feel weak again. I wonder if I'll wake up tomorrow, he thought. Groggy from the blood loss and wine, he drifted into a deep sleep.

Carlin was worried. Thoughts circled around his brain like the hand of a clock: *Maybe he had cut a nerve ... Why did he use a bungee cord ...? A tourniquet was one of the worst things he could have done .... Of course, he was a soldier. If you bleed, you put on a tourniquet ... I should have seen that coming. His arm may be black in two days.*

Carlin phoned Fenwick with five questions for Yazykov. He forwarded his office phone to his cellular phone and went home. He had promised to take his daughters skating in the Boston Commons, and while they zipped around the rink, he waited for his mobile phone to ring. No one called. He took his daughters home and tucked them into bed. "It would be a good idea," he told them, "to put Viktor in your prayers." Later that evening, he told his wife: "I might lose this guy tonight."

Fenwick sent Carlin's questions to Yazykov's boat at 10:53 p.m. and waited for a response. Nothing.

He sent another message an hour later. And then another. And then two more.

"VIKTOR: ARE YOU GETTING MY MESSAGES?? PLEASE RESPOND TO THE 5 QUESTIONS!!!!! ARE YOU OK?"

At sunup, Yazykov opened his eyes. The cabin was a mess. The smell of blood filled his nostrils. The sun breathed life into his power system, and he turned on his laptop. He had ten e-mails.

"I am OK," he replied to the ROC's urgent messages. "The hand is still sleepy, getting strength back very slowly. Thank you very much for your help. Some more later. No sun, no power. Sorry."

A day or so later, when his strength had returned, he checked his boat's position. While he was performing his surgery and sleeping, with the tiller lashed and the boat sailing itself, he had covered 239 miles, the best 24-hour run in the fleet that day. "You are perfect, little boat," he said.

Nothing But Trouble

CHAPTER EIGHT

There it is, a cold front. His eyes glued to his laptop screen, Giovanni Soldini studied the latest forecast, pondering the front's shape and direction. He was past the doldrums now, past the bulge of Brazil and heading south into the more dependable trade winds of the South Atlantic. Yes, maybe this was an opening, he thought. Maybe now he could get back on track.

It had been a rotten race so far for Soldini. After heading east out of Charleston and getting stuck behind Hurricane Lisa, he spent five tedious days floating through the doldrums. Now, after four weeks, here he was, one of the favorites to win, one of the most experienced skippers in the fleet, in one of the fastest and most expensive boats, plodding along more than 400 miles behind the leader. Sure, he had taken a gamble at the start, but his sailing strategy had never been to take the most direct route. He had been taught by Pierre Lasnier, a French weather specialist, to let the winds determine the best course, and above all, sail around high pressure systems, even if it meant adding miles.

As he studied the new forecasts on his computer, he knew that after the cold front passed over him, he would be stuck in a windless high pressure zone. The front would hit him first and then the leaders. If he stayed ahead of it, he could ride it

south and then use the westerly trade winds of the Southern Ocean as a catapult to Cape Town. If he fell behind it ... well, he decided that this possibility would not happen. He powered up his boat, adding sails, maybe flying too many at times. He stormed south, riding the front's winds, his boat slamming through the waves at fifteen knots, twenty knots, sometimes faster.

He covered an average of 360 miles per day over three days. In one 24-hour period, he sailed 386.9 nautical miles, a record for a singlehanded monohull. Slowly, he closed the gap, coming within fifty-four miles of Josh Hall and 200 miles of Isabelle Autissier, who was leading the race.

The cold front moved south, and to stay ahead of it, Soldini rode it like a surfer down the coast of South America, while the leaders charged to the east toward Africa. He was adding miles to his voyage, but he had to stay with the wind. Then, like a wave hitting a beach, the front began to peter out. He floated over the mid-Atlantic Ridge, a great underwater mountain range between Africa and South America. He knew this area often killed cold fronts. The winds began to die. His boat slowed. Meanwhile, the others were in a new weather system and flying toward Cape Town. Damn their luck, Soldini thought, they have a straight shot and I'm stuck. He was run-

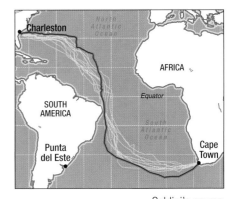

Soldini's course

Robin Davie on *South Carolina*

ning out of time.

"The big problem is that the gap is growing quickly and so close to the finish line," he said in a message to the ROC on October 29. "...Right now I am very worried."

Robin Davie thought he had finally put the puzzle together. He had fixed most everything he could on *South Carolina*, and it was finally living up to its potential, skimming across the waves like a speedboat, its wake generating a wide carpet of bubbles and spray. After crossing the equator, he closed the gap between his main Class Two rivals, J.P. Mouligne, Mike Garside and Brad Van Liew. It had been an exhausting battle to get his boat up to snuff while racing. Curled in his sleeping bag, Davie spent every night on the floor or outside in the boat's cockpit. Sleeping in these places instead of the bunk gave him a better feel for the boat. He felt a deep sense of satisfaction as *South Carolina* cut through the waves. In the last two races, his boat was a mule, the slowest in the fleet. Now, finally, he had a thoroughbred.

At about 3:00 a.m. on October 30, Davie was on the cabin floor sleeping when *South Carolina* suddenly rounded up. The change in motion woke him up. He heard the sails flogging. He climbed into his foul-weather gear - jacket, trousers and boots - grabbed a flashlight and went outside. It was windy, and ten-foot waves were knocking the boat around like schoolyard bullies. Spray was everywhere. Davie tweaked the sails and turned the tiller, but the boat didn't respond. He went to the stern and looked at the rudder. It was dark and he couldn't see much, but he didn't notice anything amiss. He tried again to steer the boat. He looked back at the stern. He had a bad feeling. It had to be the rudder.

When confronted by a particularly difficult or dangerous challenge, Davie liked to make tea. He went below, boiled some water and made a cup of PG Tips, his favorite, adding a couple of spoonfuls of sugar. He drank it and relaxed, eventually dozing off. At dawn, he climbed back outside and went to the stern. Suddenly, like a cold slap, a wave dunked him. Sopping, he held on till the wave lifted the stern. What he saw - or didn't see - felt like another slap. He had no rudder. "Another race gone," he told the waves.

Davie went below and made more tea. He considered his options as his yacht bobbed in the waves like a piece of driftwood. He could try to use his sails and turn west and head for South America. Or he could make for the tiny volcanic islands of Tristan da Cunha midway between South America and Africa, population 280. Neither choice seemed acceptable. It would be a battle to get to South America, and finding boat repair facilities on Tristan da Cunha didn't seem like such a good bet. Either way, he wouldn't get to Cape Town in time for the restart of the second leg and would be disqualified. He decided to keep heading for Africa and make the best of it.

Davie started thinking about windsurfers. Sailboards have no rudders, and windsurfers turn using only their weight and sails. He imagined his boat as a fifty-foot sailboard and soon had a plan. He adjusted his sails and grabbed four 100-foot ropes. At the end of one, he tied some anchor chain. On another he tied some netting. He let them go from the boat's stern, two lines dragging from the right and two from the left, like four tails on a kite. If he wanted to turn right, he would put all the lines on the right side and the extra drag would steer South Carolina in that direction.

It was backbreaking work, lifting the lines from one side of the boat, over the useless rudder shaft, to the other side. But the system worked. One day he covered 165 miles, more miles than some of the fleet's slower boats. He pushed hard, knowing that he would need every minute in Cape Town to finish all the repairs. He configured the sails in ways that he knew added stress to the rig. He watched the forestay pump back and forth when the boat slammed through the waves. After six days, the pounding was too much and the forestay snapped. The mast was in danger, so he slowed his pace. As he fixed

the forestay, he found himself in a high pressure system. Gone was the wind that had made his windsurfing model work. Without any drag, the boat behaved like an angry two-year-old, steering in any direction but the one Davie wanted. When the boat went off course, Davie spent an hour tuning the sails and moving the dragging ropes. Five minutes later, the boat was heading in a different direction. "Bastard thing!" Davie would say. The repetition was exhausting. Trim the sails, move the lines. Nap, wake up and find the boat off course, trim the sails, move the lines ... One sorry day he spent an hour trying to get back on course only to find that he had lost a mile. In twenty-four hours, he logged only twenty-nine miles. He felt as if he had been sentenced to hard labor. He turned off his mind, trying not to think about what he was doing. He slept in fifteen-minute intervals. The boat wouldn't let him sleep any longer. Every time his eyes shut, *South Carolina* went off course. "Bastard thing! This is torture."

In a satellite phone interview with a reporter from *The Post and Courier* in Charleston, he said, "Sometimes the boat seems as if it's totally possessed. It wants to go the wrong way all the time. If you put your head down for some sleep, you wake up to the ropes banging and crashing." The whole experience was worse than when he lost his mast 1,600 miles from Cape Horn in the 1994-95 BOC Challenge. "It makes you go bloody, stark raving mad, absolutely nuts," Davie said.

What had he done to deserve this? It was as if the world was conspiring against him. As he dipped into the Southern Ocean, big black clouds hung over his yacht for days, pelting him with cold rain. Then, his mainsail suffered a thirty-foot tear from the leech to the luff. His cold fingers went to work, stitching it back together. His computer got damp and started misbehaving. With no wind, he was still hundreds of miles from Cape Town, running out of food and losing weight.

Robin Davie

Racing To Table Mountain

CHAPTER NINE

Isabelle Autissier knew she was in the Southern Ocean when she saw her first albatross. With their ten-foot wing spans, they are the largest seabirds in the world. They play with the waves, diving toward the swells, tearing along the trough and straightening their wings at the last minute for maximum lift, using the draft from the crest as an extra boost. These great birds are the singlehanded sailors of the sky, flying for days at a time at an average pace of 18 mph, sleeping on the wing. Some have circumnavigated the globe several times, cruising with the Southern Ocean's westerly winds and currents.

On October 24, the clouds broke, and Autissier sailed under blue skies toward Cape Town, about 1,000 miles to the east. This far south, the light had a golden tint that contrasted sharply with the cold blue seas. Despite her broken forestay, she was in first place. But Marc Thiercelin, the quiet French skipper, and Mike Golding, the ex-British firefighter, were close by, riding the same low pressure system spinning east, so Autissier flew as many sails as she could.

Golding also pushed his boat, knowing the finish in Cape Town would be close and that the weather probably would decide who won. "For three days *PRB* and *Team Group 4* have been sailing on the edge of the high pressure," Golding

reported to the ROC on October 30. "Cloud and rain behind us and beautiful azure blue sky ahead. This has controlled our speed." If they went too fast, he continued, they would sail into lighter breeze. Too slow, and the front would push them forward anyway.

Golding was a short and stocky man with a round face, close-cropped hair, and a love of numbers. He started sailing when he was nine years old and made his first circumnavigation when he was eighteen. A year later he became a firefighter, and quickly moved up the ranks, eventually heading a watch of seventeen men and four engines. It was good practice for a skipper-to-be. In 1992, he and his crew placed second in the British Steel Challenge, a race around the world from east to west, sometimes called the "wrong way" because boats face the tough westerly winds of the Southern Ocean. In 1996, he and his crew won the BT Global Challenge, another crewed round-the-world race. The British press pegged Golding as the country's best bet to dethrone the French singlehanded stars.

A tidy and analytical person, Golding had charts and formulas that determined when and what kind of sails to put up in certain winds, directions and seas. "I like to sail by the numbers if I can," he once said. "It's more efficient." He collected

Marc Thiercelin on *SOMEWHERE* finishes in Cape Town

every bit of information on the weather he could, crunched the numbers, digested them. And as the fleet neared Cape Town, he calculated that a high pressure system ahead would move north. His formula was correct. In his message to the ROC, he wrote: "The wind shift I have waited for came, and I knew I had gotten it first - Brilliant!" When the wind picked up, he watched *Team Group 4* clock thirty knots before a jibe knocked it on its side.

Autissier saw Golding's move on the position updates beamed to the fleet and knew she was beaten. "I no longer have any hope of catching him," she told the ROC on October 30, a day before making landfall. "I will probably arrive five hours behind him, or a little more. That's no big deal, and it's not a big handicap in the context of a round-the-world race." Considering that she couldn't fly all her sails because of the broken forestay, she was satisfied with her performance. "I don't know how I could have done better."

Golding sailed into Cape Town's Table Bay the morning of October 31. The deep blue Atlantic waters sparkled in the sun. Table Mountain loomed ahead. Then the winds died. He changed sails and puttered forward with every gust. Just before the finish, the winds kicked up again, and he streaked across the line after 34 days, 18 hours, and 19 minutes at sea. It was the fastest first leg in the race's history, eclipsing Autissier's

record run in the 1994-95 race by 13 hours. Golding also was the first British skipper to win any leg in the race's history. When he stepped off *Team Group 4*, he grinned. "I'm over the moon."

Three hours later, Autissier crossed the line, her earrings glittering in the late afternoon sun. A rugby match was going on at the time, and when *PRB* reached the harbor, people rushed out of the bars with their beers and cheered. When she stepped onto the docks, Golding handed her a bouquet of flowers and gave her a hug. "We had to fight every minute," she told reporters, laughing. "It is not an easy game as these guys are very clever with the weather. So they don't make any mistakes."

Two hours after Autissier made it in, race officials spotted her countryman, Marc Thiercelin, off the horizon, thundering toward Cape Town at a twenty-two-knot clip. He flew his torn and tattered mainsail and genoa. "They looked like the suit of sails employed on Kevin Costner's trimaran in *Waterworld*," Herb McCormick, the race's media correspondent, remarked. As the sun sank behind Table Mountain, Thiercelin crossed the finish line. As if on cue, a 50-mph gust swept through, and Thiercelin's Kevlar mainsail exploded into six pieces. "I'm a lucky man," Thiercelin said to himself.

Lucky but not happy. Thiercelin wearily stepped off the docks. He was disappointed with his third-place finish. A few reporters peppered him with questions. Looking shell-shocked, he declined to say anything at first. Later he told McCormick that Leg One was "my toughest voyage ever."

British skipper Josh Hall arrived two days later, all grins. Remembering his disastrous race in 1994, when his boat sank after colliding with a metal container, he told reporters "I'm glad to have arrived on my own, on my own boat and in contention."

The next morning was misty and gray as Soldini steered *FILA* across the line. Soldini's mood seemed to reflect the weather. He was three days behind Golding and in fifth place.

When Soldini stepped off the dock, he looked weary and deflated. McCormick asked him for his thoughts. "I really wanted to arrive," he said. "I've had enough."

But then his family and friends smothered him with hugs and congratulations. Their presence seemed like a salve to his sore mood, and soon the clouds lifted, the sun shone, and Soldini was walking around the docks, laughing as usual, with the daughter of an assistant slung over his shoulder.

Fedor Konioukhov, meanwhile, was in the middle of the Atlantic, battling for every mile. His autopilots had quit, and he spent hours on deck tuning his sails, skipping meals and sleep. The boat was still taking on water, and Konioukhov pumped about fifty gallons overboard every day to keep it under control. The waves were huge with small waves on top of larger swells. The Russian adventurer nicknamed the waves "mother and baby." He noticed a tiny sea bird drop a small fish on the deck every morning. Each time, Konioukhov threw the fish back. This happened five days in a row, and the Russian was moved deeply by the ritual.

"I think that this bird wanted to help me by feeding me," he said in a message to the ROC on November 12. "In the past couple of days I was in really bad situation, too much physical work, no time to cook, and when this morning this small sea bird brought her gift again and dropped it on the bow, I cried a little for such human care."

The next day, a whale surfaced thirty feet from his boat, close enough for him to see its eyes. The whale disappeared, and Konioukhov tried to imagine what sounds and music it was making. A week later, after steering for two hours, he went below to make some coffee and peel off his wet clothes. Suddenly, he felt the boat hit something, a thud not a crack. A chill went down his back. Another whale! Then, a few seconds later, he felt another thud. He rushed onto the deck and saw the beast. It was larger than his sixty-foot yacht. Another chill.

The keel! He scrambled down below to check the keel bolts. They seemed solid. He breathed a sigh of relief. Had he been perpendicular to the whale and hit, he could have been in real trouble.

"Everybody knows that I am not a racer," he said in a message to the ROC. "A couple days before the start in Charleston, one skipper in Class One promised me a lot of new experience from being in the race. I definitely don't need that kind of experience."

In early November, the other racers began to trickle into Cape Town. Just after midnight November 6, J.P. Mouligne was fifty miles away when he saw the glow of the city. As dawn broke, he saw the flat top of Table Mountain appear off the horizon. As he neared the coast, the mountain seemed to grow out of the ocean.

Mouligne crossed the line after forty days and twelve hours at sea, the best showing ever for a sailor in a fifty-footer and the first of the race's Class Two skippers to make it in. During a press conference he told reporters about a knockdown in which he found himself hanging onto his boom, chest-deep in the water. "The boat was falling over me." He had on his safety harness. "But it was very scary." A reporter asked what was the worst moment of the race. Mouligne said it was the night Mike Garside called him on the radio.

"I was down below and Mike calls on the radio. He talks to me for a while, then says to go on deck. I go up, and there he is sailing almost beside me. It was a terrible moment. He was pushing hard to pass me and I was just not going to let it happen."

By the time Mouligne arrived in Cape Town, he and Garside weren't the best of friends. Midway, after Mouligne made several maneuvers that extended his lead, Garside sent an e-mail to the ROC, which posted it on the race's Web site.

"Three times since the start I've been suckered by a foxy

Mouligne

Garside

Van Liew

Van Liew on *Balance Bar*

frog . . . Behind the cool, charming Gaelic exterior of Monsieur Mouligne there lurks a mind that is devious in the extreme. To take me for a sucker three times is too much. The gloves are off! Mouligne is proving to be a tough nut to crack, but crack him I promise to do."

Mouligne was offended by the frog reference and thought about zapping back an e-mail saying such comments weren't in the race's spirit. But he let it go. He used it as motivation to sail harder.

Garside finished the next day at dawn, declaring that he despised sailing more than ever. Brad Van Liew crossed an hour and seven minutes later. Garside and Mouligne climbed aboard Van Liew's boat as it was tied up and embraced him. "Man, this guy really gave me headaches," Garside told the crowd. For the first time, Van Liew revealed that his rudder bearings had worn out in the South Atlantic, and that he had been forced to steer using only his sails. His performance was one of the biggest surprises of the race. *Balance Bar* was an older, and presumably slower boat than Mouligne's and Garside's new Finot yachts. But Van Liew had been a contender throughout the leg, even without a working rudder.

The other American in the race, George Stricker, made it in a week later after a mostly problem-free sail aboard *Rapscallion III*. Then, on November 16, relieved race officials greeted Viktor Yazykov on a cloudy afternoon. His socks and deck shoes still had brown stains from his bloody evening under the knife. Yazykov flashed a smile, showing his gold teeth. A group of Russians cheered. His elbow looked fine but still hurt. At a press conference, he winced as he picked up a Champagne bottle. "I can write and use a spoon but it's difficult," he said, holding up his hand and pointing to his ring and little fingers. "These two fingers are OK, but these two (pointer and index) are not very good. I had a small problem before I reached Charleston and the doctor there told me to rest it. But when you are trying to put a reef in during a Force Ten, how can you take care?"

Neal Petersen was next, and the afternoon of November 17, the waterfront's piers were lined with friends, spectators and schoolchildren, including classes from Petersen's old high school. Minoru Saito crossed the line a few days later early in the morning, sighing. "Very bad problems." Midway in the race, his autopilot had conked out. "So for almost five weeks, I hand steer. Crazy," he said throwing his hands up in exasperation.

When Robin Davie arrived after fifty-eight frustrating days at sea, someone handed him some ice cream and a container of milk, and he wolfed them down. Looking almost as thin as a concentration camp survivor, Davie had run out of food a day before. He arrived with only a jar of Dijon mustard and a bottle containing a few drops of Worcestershire sauce. Despite his battle to steer the boat and his hunger, he appeared relaxed. "So nice to be here," he said between slurps.

On November 26, Neil Hunter slipped in after sixty-one days aboard his small and slow yacht, *Paladin II*. In last place, Fedor Konioukhov was still struggling to finish before the disqualification deadline. Racers had to be in by noon November 28, a week before the restart, and race officials privately were betting that Konioukhov wouldn't make it. Concerned that Konioukhov's campaign was too disorganized, some even hoped he would miss the deadline, knowing that the Southern Ocean legs would be even more challenging and dangerous.

But a strong and steady southeasterly wind rushed to the Russian's rescue, blowing him toward Cape Town at speeds he hadn't seen throughout the race. He made it across the finish line with just ten hours to spare. "Long trip," he said, shaking his head. "Very, very long trip." A reporter asked how this compared with his other expeditions. "On Mount Everest, you watch the weather. In Around Alone, you must also watch the clock," he replied. "On that mountain, the greatest danger extends over a two-week period, as you prepare to make the summit. On this race the danger is for two months. And that is just on Leg One. Compared to Everest, this is very difficult."

Into Africa

CHAPTER TEN

Late November is springtime in South Africa, and one warm afternoon a week after his arrival, Neal Petersen drove with a television crew to his childhood home. It was in a modest neighborhood on the outskirts of Cape Town. He motioned toward a syringa tree that his father had planted. "This was my dream tree," he said. As a boy, he built a tree house in its branches, imagining the bits of wood were planks on the deck of a great sailing ship. He swung from a rope, pretending he was a pirate. He climbed nets as if he were a sailor tending the topsails. At the top, he built a crow's nest and surveyed the neighborhood. He spent hours alone in his leafy ship, reading books about the sea, dreaming of adventure. Now, more than twenty years later, the tree was older and smaller than it seemed when he was child, and as Petersen spoke to the television crew underneath it, a thought flashed through his mind, part dream, part reality. He imagined he was a successful sailor returning to his very first boat, now in a museum but still in ship shape.

Petersen was feeling good about this race. He had few problems during his voyage from Charleston. This was a breakthrough. For most of his sailing career, he had battled one misfortune after another. In one race, he collided with a freighter and poked a hole in his boat, forcing him to bail his way across the Atlantic. On another voyage, a boom smashed his forehead and he was forced to use a clothespin to stop the bleeding. Then he collided with a shipping container, lost his rudder and almost starved until an Irish fishing vessel rescued him. During the 1994-95 BOC Challenge, a storm off South Africa turned his yacht upside down, tearing off his mast and forcing him to quit. After retiring from that race, he vowed to finish the next one. He sailed to Charleston and spent the next three years there fixing his boat, lining up small sponsorship deals and setting up the nonprofit No Barriers Education Foundation.

With missionary zeal, he traveled across the country to schools, boardrooms and government offices, preaching his message: "Never give up your dreams" and "In life there are no barriers, only solutions." Like a politician running for office, he wasn't shy about asking for money. He turned his life's story into a marketing tool. At the ripe age of twenty-seven, he published his autobiography. In 1998, he produced a coloring book featuring his adventures. He was a relentless salesman, too much for some people's taste, and some of his fellow skippers snickered and rolled their eyes during his speeches, saying privately that Petersen's talents lay in self-promotion, not sailing. Some also scoffed at his boat. No mistaking this for one

Neal Petersen

Neal Petersen on *www.no-barriers.com*

of the new Finot rockets, Petersen's boat was round and fat in the middle, like a pregnant fish. He built it himself in 1990 in South Africa. Not only was it one of the oldest boats in the race, it was the smallest, just thirty-eight feet long when he first launched it. Later, he added two feet to the stern so it would comply with race rules, which mandated a minimum length of forty feet.

Even though Petersen had a small, home-built boat with a funny shape, he was ahead of four larger and supposedly faster boats when he sailed into Cape Town. Petersen hoped his performance would silence his critics. But some said the hardest part of the race was yet to come and continued to be irritated by Petersen's speeches at press conferences and other functions. Brad Van Liew made a side bet that Petersen and his little red boat wouldn't make it to New Zealand.

Petersen was used to naysayers, though. After all, he had grown up in South Africa. Under the country's apartheid system, Petersen was classified as colored, of mixed racial back-

ground. As a boy, he was thrown off whites-only beaches. As a young man, he couldn't travel in white areas without a pass and was kicked out of restaurants when he entered with white friends. It was an evil system that tore his family apart. When apartheid was created in the 1940s, his grandmother had darker skin and was deemed colored. His grandmother's brother was classified white. Brother and sister no longer could eat, travel or live together.

Petersen also had been born with a deformed hip and spent much of his early childhood in hospitals. He couldn't run and kick balls like his friends, so he immersed himself in books, especially sea stories. His father taught him how to swim, sometimes taking him into the wild waters off Cape Point where the Indian and Atlantic oceans meet. Several operations helped the hip condition, and as a young teen, he started hanging around yacht clubs, not exactly bastions of racial progressivism. He nevertheless managed to persuade yachtsmen to take him out on sails and eventually hire him as crew. One day in 1982, when he was fourteen, he bumped into Richard Broadhead on the docks of the Royal Cape Yacht Club. Broadhead had just finished Leg One of the first BOC Challenge. Fascinated by the man and his quest to round Cape Horn, Petersen declared that he, too, would sail alone around the world. His school friends snickered when he shared his dream. Petersen later became a professional diver for a diamond company, vacuuming the gemstones from gravel on the sea bed off the coast of Namibia. He earned enough money to build his own yacht, naming it *Stella-R* after his mother. For the Around Alone, he renamed the boat *www.no-barriers.com* and painted a big black-and-white number one on the hull.

The boat and its thirty-one-year-old captain had held together beautifully on the way to Africa. No leaks, no missing rudders, no destroyed masts, no bleeding foreheads. During the voyage, Petersen felt a deep sense of solitude that left him both melancholy and full of joy. He knew he didn't really belong in Charleston, a city kind to visitors but slow to accept those who linger. He no longer felt like he fit in South Africa, with its bubbling racial problems and politics. No, he thought, the sea was where he felt most at home and at peace.

On Sunday, November 29, the Cape Doctor arrived, a powerful southeasterly wind, so-called because it cleared the city of pollution and insects. Petersen spent the bright afternoon taking his boat out for a photo shoot. Later that evening, he went to the Royal Cape Yacht Club for a race function. He was late, and he flew through the doors. He had been a member of the club in the past and soon saw some friends. As he was saying hello, another member named David Bongers sidled up to him, put his arm on his shoulder and said, "It's good to have our *hotnot* back in town again."

Petersen was stunned. In America, only one word packed the same kind of gunpowder: nigger. Bongers saw Petersen's frown and said he was only joking. Petersen replied that he didn't appreciate that kind of humor. Fuming, he turned his back on Bongers.

The slur broke Petersen's sense of serenity, and he spent the next week trying to deal with that fracture. "I see some improvements in my country, but I feel it still has a long way to go," he told friends a few days later while sitting in his boat's cockpit, the Cape Doctor still rattling his rigging. "I'm ready for the race to start. I know there are a lot of good people in this country, and I want to focus on them and not waste my energy on negative things. But I'm not going to take it anymore. I'm not going to let people get away with this kind of thing. Times have changed. I've changed."

Indeed, momentous changes were sweeping through Petersen's country. In 1992, South Africa began to dismantle the laws of apartheid, eventually electing Nelson Mandela president in 1994. Poor rural South Africans, hoping that the political changes would lead to better living conditions, moved from the arid African bush to Cape Town and other large urban cities, crowding into townships by the millions. Residents lived in closet-sized shacks with corrugated metal roofs. These townships stretched for miles. The violent crime rate, especially in the townships, was among the highest in the world. The country also had been rocked by revelations from the Truth and Reconciliation Commission, set up to identify incidents of racial violence and injustice during apartheid. The city was a tinderbox.

When Paul Mare, commodore of the Royal Cape Yacht Club, heard about the slur, he knew it meant trouble. He called for an immediate inquiry. "We clearly don't condone these kinds of statements, and it's sad they could undo all the very hard work that many people had done at the club," Mare said before the panel took up Petersen's complaint. "This is going to create a lot of ill will when the news gets out."

The club expelled Bongers, a member of a prominent Cape Town sailing family, and the dispute landed on the front pages of the city's newspapers. In one article, Bongers said he had only been joking. "I'm honestly not a racist," he told the *Saturday Argus.* "The political changes of the past few years are the best thing that have ever happened in the country."

The slur added tension to an already strained relationship between the Cape Town sailing community and the Around Alone. In the previous four races, the Royal Cape Yacht Club had hosted the event. But race organizers, hoping for more visibility and foot traffic, decided to station the fleet at the Victoria and Alfred Waterfront, a shining, massive new harbor development a mile away from the yacht club. It had become the city's main tourist attraction. "We feel we have been marginalized by commercialism," Mare said a few days before the restart. "There's a lot of ill feelings, not against the event, but against the decision to move the race to a more commercial venue."

The Around Alone fleet was tied up next to a pier at the far end of the Victoria and Alfred Waterfront. It was a pleasant set-

Fedor Konioukhov makes repairs in Cape Town

ting. Beyond the breakwater were the blue waters of Table Bay and beyond, the Cape of Good Hope. Toward the northeast was Table Mountain, the city's defining landmark, a craggy, flat-topped peak that sometimes had a white layer of cloud - nicknamed the tablecloth - rolling off its side. Developers had converted old shipping piers into a huge hotel and shopping mall filled with theaters, chain stores and fast-food restaurants. Music by AC/DC blared out of the Hard Rock Cafe, and tourists and residents mingled in the food court, lining up for Kentucky Fried Chicken buckets. The waterfront had a distinctly American flavor, too American for some. Four months before, a bomb had exploded in the Planet Hollywood restaurant, killing three people and injuring twenty-seven others. Police believed that the bombers were a militant Muslim gang angry about U.S. air strikes in Iraq. (On New Year's Day, three weeks after the Around Alone fleet left for Auckland, another bomb would explode near the entrance to a mall, injuring three more people.) Despite the bombing, the waterfront was a lively and festive place with pleasure boaters sharing the harbor with working tugs, ferries, fishing vessels and the sleek and delicate boats of the Around Alone. Concerts were held daily in an amphitheater near the main food court. The Around Alone yachts added a new spice to the mix, and thousands of tourists and residents strolled down the pier to watch the crews and skippers prepare for the next leg.

Not all the yachts were at the pier, though. Four days before the restart, Fedor Konioukhov's yacht rested on a cradle next to a row of restaurants and shops, looking like a ten-story sailboat monument. Koniouhhov had taken it out of the water to fix the keel and some other problems. On the right side of the hull, paint had been scraped off where the whale banged into the boat. Below, in the yacht's shadow, Konioukhov and his son, Oscar, chatted with a man hired to fix a rudder problem. A reporter from a large Moscow newspaper stood nearby. Konioukhov's last place finish had triggered a big debate in Russia. Some had said Konioukhov did a poor job representing their nation. Oscar, a student, was quick to come this father's defense.

"He'll never come in first, but he was the only man who could sail and find the money. Maybe he's a worse sailor, but he's here. And besides, coming in last isn't so bad. Everyone talks about you, and that's good for our sponsor."

Giovanni Soldini's performance also generated a heated discussion in his native Italy. While his shore crew readied his yacht, he flew to Italy for a press conference. "Everyone was saying I was stupid and that I should have done this, I should have done that, or look at what Paul Cayard did in the Whitbread, how he controlled the others. One guy told me how to do the race." Soldini couldn't believe the arrogance of his country's media. "They should sail and then talk." The more he thought about his choices in Leg One, the more he believed that his luck had simply been bad. He was convinced that his strategy of letting the wind and sea determine his course was the way to go. Despite the criticism, he felt surprisingly calm going into Leg Two. "I was Zen," he would say later.

Meanwhile, the race's leader, Mike Golding, basked in the publicity. Before the race, Golding considered the Around Alone a mere dress rehearsal for the Vendee Globe, which he deemed the pinnacle of singlehanded sailing races. But over time, the Around Alone became an obsession. He enjoyed the fraternal feelings between the skippers and shore crews. In Leg One, he showed that he could beat the best singlehanded sailors in the world. He had an amazing boat and a sponsor with deep pockets. For the Around Alone, he had a budget of more than $1.2 million, not including his million-dollar yacht. Yeah, he thought, I can win this race. He put the Vendee Globe out of his mind.

The fleet would leave for Auckland, New Zealand, on December 5, and the week before the restart was a harried time. Crews readied sails, coiled ropes, stocked food. No one was busier than Robin Davie. When he limped into Cape Town without a rudder, he also learned that his mast had cracked.

Two friends from Charleston, Ned Stender and Bill Scott, flew to Cape Town to help, working from dawn until midnight on the rudder, mast, and a laundry list of other repairs. Between cigarettes, Davie gulped liters of whole milk, trying to gain back some of the weight he lost on Leg One. His boat was full of tools, tape, springs and buckets. Down below, wires and lines were thrown about like spilled spaghetti. Just as had happened in Charleston, Davie was racing against the clock, not sure if he was going to leave with the fleet.

Indeed, as the Cape Doctor continued to pound the city, a feeling of tension swept through the docks. Minoru Saito sat one night in a tent overlooking the boats, drinking beer with Julie Weston, another visitor from Charleston. The winds howled and the tent shook as Saito told a story about how he had been in Cape Town the year before, and how one night he fell asleep and Harry Mitchell appeared to him in a dream. He and Mitchell had sailed together in the last race and were in the same storm when Mitchell was lost at sea. In his dream, Saito asked: "Who's next?" and Mitchell responded, "Why, Minoru, it's you."

Imagine the planet is a big blender, and you're making a margarita. Turn the blender on. At the bottom, everything is churning and chopping and spinning the fastest. That's the Southern Ocean. You won't find this sea on many maps. It is a nickname of sorts for the body of water between Antarctica and the tips of South America, Australia and Africa. It is a wild and massive void where the average wave is the size of a two-story house. Uninterrupted by any large land mass, powerful currents whip around the globe. Sometimes the waves run in great long lines, one after another, evenly spaced like a giant piece of corduroy. Other times, the waves come from different directions, great moving mounds that slam into each other like Sumo wrestlers. One weather depression after another moves east with these currents, whipping the seas into a froth that

Robin Davie works on rudder

sometimes makes it look as if the water is smoking. It has been estimated that one wave in 300,000 can reach a height of 120 feet. Farther south, where the westerly winds are steadiest, chunks of ice called growlers bob in the waves. Most of the Around Alone takes place in this frigid arena, which some have dubbed the "Liquid Himalayas."

Robin Davie had been in the Southern Ocean twice before and had seen storms whip the waves into foamy fifty-foot castles of water, felt the sting of snowflakes caught in hurricane-force winds, as if someone had hurled millions of needles into the air.

The morning of the restart, he was busy at work on his boat. He was in no mood to sail an unprepared boat into the teeth of the Southern Ocean. "I have everything to lose by leaving today, and everything to gain by leaving a day or two later well prepared." His decision to wait a few days seemed to lift

Cape Town the night before the restart

would force them to sail too hard and damage the boats. "I think if we sail as hard on the second leg as we did on the first, there's going to be a helluva lot of damage and someone is going to wipe out," Josh Hall had said earlier in the week. "These boats can be lethal. They all have very similar boat speeds. Some of the skippers are prepared to take more risks with their boats than I am. Giovanni, for instance, has a deserved reputation for being quite a cavalier, gung-ho skipper. When you're like that, you either win or you have a spectacular accident."

In some ways, the competition in the Around Alone was more intense than in the nonstop Vendee Globe. In the Vendee, skippers had to pace themselves and hold back somewhat, knowing that even a minor repair requiring a stop would force them out of the race. But because of the Around Alone's three stops, skippers could push their boats a little harder. They could take the boats to the edge of their design capabilities. Where that edge was, however, no one knew for sure.

The Finot boats were designed specifically for the Around Alone and Vendee Globe. Made of lightweight carbon fiber, their saucer-shaped hulls were just one quarter-inch thick. Because the hulls were so thin, the skippers could feel the coldness of the water on the cabin floor and had to wear special insulated boots. The cabins were cramped and Spartan spaces, no wood paneling or fancy brass fixtures. Bunks were on each side. J.P. Mouligne always slept on the windward bunk, hoping that the extra weight might add a pinch of speed. "It makes me feel like I'm working while I'm asleep," he said. Isabelle Autissier preferred to sleep at her chart table, which was shaped like a pair of wings to compensate for the heel of the boat. Some of the skippers had toilets. Others merely used buckets. Adding to the prison-like atmosphere was the graffiti and drawings on the hull walls done by the skippers and their friends. In Autissier's *PRB*, the designers sketched the skyline of La Rochelle. Mouligne's walls were covered with people's

his spirits. He smiled more often and the lines in his face seemed less sharp.

As Davie paced around his boat, about 250 people lined the pier, watching orange rubber rafts with powerful twin outboards wait to pull the Around Alone yachts from the docks. Isabelle Autissier went from boat to boat, giving each skipper a hug. She had a serious look on her face. "You never go into the Southern Ocean with a smile," she would say later.

The race was shaping up as the most competitive in the event's history. Going into Leg Two, just three days separated leader Mike Golding from fifth-place skipper Giovanni Soldini. Soldini would have to sail hard and smart to move up. All five Class One front-runners had similar boats, designed by Groupe Finot of France. They were wide, striking vessels designed specifically for the Southern Ocean's steady westerly blast. All five skippers were a little concerned that the competition signatures and expressions of encouragement. During the race's next two legs, skippers would spend most of their time in these spare and primitive quarters because it was too uncomfortable to go outside.

But what most set these boats apart from other sailboats was their widths. The beam on Soldini's *FILA* was almost nineteen feet. The extra width made these boats more stable sailing downwind in the Southern Ocean's great swells. Skippers liked to compare them to giant windsurfers or surfboards. The wider the beam, though, the less likely a boat was able to right itself after a knockdown. In general, wider boats also had a tendency to keep rolling and capsize. Upside down, the mast acts like a giant keel, and it is almost impossible to right the boat. Only one person, Giovanni Soldini, had managed to right a capsized sixty-foot Finot. That had happened during his tragic attempt to break the transatlantic speed record before the race. Mouligne, fearing a capsize, installed air bags on the back of his fifty-foot Finot-designed *Cray Valley.* The theory was that if a boat turned over, the air bags could inflate, breaking the suction of the deck from the water and making it easy to flip the boat back over. Autissier had planned to have a similar setup, but she had an installation problem at the start and left them off. On the stern of her boat and the other Finots was an escape hatch, a vivid reminder of the capsize potential of these fast yachts. Indeed, these boats were among the most unusual wind-driven vessels ever built - boats designed to all but sail themselves through monstrous seas at speeds of twenty knots or more with the expectation that waves will knock them on their sides - and the hope that they'll pop back up for another round.

"You know," Soldini said one afternoon, "the architects don't really know what happens to these boats in the middle of the sea. It's not like a plane, where they build a piece, break it, and then measure it so they know how much stress it takes to break it. In a boat like this, they take a book and say 'Hmmm, OK, two tons, it will break at two tons.' The numbers they

come up with, it's just a joke."

The morning of the start, Mike Golding was up at six o'-clock, poring over the latest weather information. He noticed a small weather system with a southwesterly wind in the Atlantic that seemed to be heading for Cape Town. He thought if he could steer into it just after the start, he might be able to make a surprise break from the pack. His campaign dispatched a helicopter later in the morning to pinpoint the weather system and gauge the strength of its winds.

As the morning wore on, the docks began to bustle with friends and shore crew saying goodbye. Neal Petersen hugged his sister as tears welled in her eyes. J.P. Mouligne and Mike Garside shook hands. "Just have a safe trip," Mouligne told his rival. Autissier was towed out first to an area just beyond the harbor's breakwater. The skies were gray and the winds were light. Above, two aerobatic planes did loops.

A half hour before the start, Golding's helicopter landed and the pilot sped out in a boat to give the skipper a briefing. It turned out that the weather system would have no effect. The skippers began their zig-zag dance to get in position. Ten minutes before the start, Giovanni Soldini lost control of his mainsail and screamed away from his rivals toward Robbins Island, where Nelson Mandela once had been imprisoned. But a few minutes later, he had everything sorted out and a single reef in his giant white mainsail.

At noon, a horn blew aboard a passenger vessel anchored at the starting line, and the race was on again. Soldini was first over the line, followed by Golding and Hall. As usual, Autissier stayed back and waited for everything to clear.

It was calm at first, but as the boats sped away, the winds grew stronger. Neil Hunter clipped into his safety harness. The fleet's fastest boats were soon slicing through the waves at an easy ten-knot clip, their bows pointing south toward Antarctica, pounding into bigger and bigger waves.

Into the Waves

CHAPTER ELEVEN

The first night, as the fleet steered into the Cape of Good Hope and past windswept Cape Point, a storm swooped in from the west, giving the skippers their first taste of the Southern Ocean. Isabelle Autissier, like the others, spent most of her time below, letting the autopilot steer while she studied the weather forecasts. *PRB's* cabin was a noisy place to live and work. When waves slapped against the carbon fiber hull they sounded like drumbeats. Mingling with these plastic, gong-like blasts was the sound of whooshing water. It was like being inside a washing machine. The boat was always in motion, and Autissier always had a grip on something. The swells traveled between twenty and thirty knots. She felt the boat accelerate as it surfed down a wave and slow when it reached the trough and plowed into the back of another one. Sometimes the waves caught up with her yacht and broke over the stern in an angry green-and-white flood. When she did venture outside to the cockpit or deck, the spray was furious, so strong sometimes that she couldn't open her eyes. Riding these big Southern Ocean waves was stressful, but it also made her feel more connected with her boat and the sea.

Inside her cabin, amid snapshots of friends and her shore team, a friend had pasted a sticker: "Wild Women Don't Get the Blues." But as she sped away from Cape Town, she still had some unpleasant memories rattling around her brain. Leg Two of the Around Alone had often been the race's most destructive stretch. It was during this leg in the 1986-87 race that the event suffered its first fatality. French skipper Jacques de Roux apparently was washed overboard off the coast of Australia. During the 1994-95 race, a monster storm pummeled the fleet. One skipper, David Adams, was thrown overboard but was saved by his six-foot lifeline. Another competitor, Steve Pettengill, had to climb the mast three times in the freezing rain, bobbing back and forth in the swells like a human metronome. When he finished the repairs, fifty-foot waves knocked his boat on its side, snapping the boom. Later a wave picked up the boat and tossed it into the air. Pettengill was in his cabin with the hatches closed. When the boat landed, it tunneled into a wave so deep that Pettengill's ears popped from the pressure. A window popped open and the water came in with the force of a fire hose. He spent a week fighting storm after storm and trying to repair their damage. One time he woke up standing, holding some tools, drooling.

In that race, a 70-mph gust also flipped over Neal Petersen's boat, snapping his mast. With the remnants, he made a makeshift rig and limped back to Cape Town. Another storm toppled Autissier's mast, but she was too far from Africa to turn

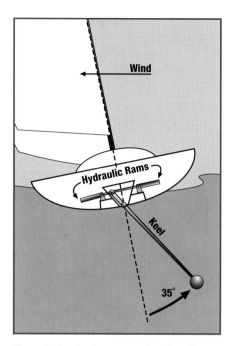

The swinging keels on several yachts allow the boats to sail with more sails up and not heel over as much.

around. "Thirty knots of wind, sea dark, sky crying," she said in a message to her French shore crew. "I'm working to clear off the deck and see what I can do. There is almost nothing left on deck. Nothing left of my dream. But I won't think about that now. I am safe." Using a spinnaker pole, she built a jury rig and sailed 1,100 miles to the Kerguelen Islands, a desolate, glacier-covered series of islands with about 100 residents and a French weather station. Her shore crew managed to ship a smaller second-hand mast to the island on a supply ship. She installed it and was soon on her way. Then another storm hit. Autissier remembered hearing the groan of a large wave approach. It picked up her boat and rolled it 360 degrees, wiping the rig from the deck and peeling off the bulbous cabin roof. She rocked in foaming seas for four days before an Australian military helicopter lifted her off the foundering boat with a winch. Later, dressed in a dry Australian navy uniform, she joked: "The colors are good for me" and then vowed that she would race again.

The morning of December 8, three days after leaving Cape Town, Autissier looked behind her chart table on the floor and noticed a loose screw on one of the keel's hydraulic arms. This was trouble. A loose keel could be a disaster. "I have to be safe," she thought and reduced her sails.

Autissier's yacht had a swinging keel. Held in place by hydraulic rams, she could move it thirty-five degrees each way to trim her boat instead of using water ballast. This made her boat lighter and, presumably, faster than boats with heavy water ballast systems.

After she added reefs to her mainsail, she picked up her satellite phone and called her shore team and the boat's designer. They assured her that one hydraulic arm was strong enough to keep the keel in place. Slowly, she flew more sails, and after two hours, she felt confident that the keel would hold. That evening, she sent a message to the ROC: "I will not

lose the keel! That's pretty good news . . . I'm fed up with these crises. I would like to make a normal leg for once!"

Leg Two was anything but normal for George Stricker, the 63-year-old retired entrepreneur from Kentucky. A day after the restart, the boom on *Rapscallion III* broke in two pieces, forcing him to steer back to Cape Town. He fixed the boom and set out once more. Then he discovered a diesel fuel leak and turned around again. All these problems had Stricker scratching his recently shaved head. His first leg had been virtually trouble free. Finally, two weeks into the race, his boom broke away from the mast in a 60-mph gale. Stricker sent an e-mail to the ROC. "Looks like the gooseneck was under built. Just an add-on part with layers of carbon and no substantial build-up of carbon. On inspection, it looked like it just peeled off." He phoned the ROC. He was turning around one last time, the second skipper to bow out. "This race is not for me," he said.

Things were far better on Giovanni Soldini's boat. Despite a bad head cold, he pushed *FILA* as hard as he dared. Three days into Leg Two, he sent a message to the ROC: "Since Sunday night we've been racing along with winds of forty to fifty knots. Every now and then a wave takes a hold of *FILA* and throws her down its face at alarming speed. The noise and vibration are deafening. It's impossible to relax even for a moment. In these conditions your muscles are ready to react to every change in the boat's trim or speed - you virtually become part of the boat itself." In another message, he said he was on the deck one late afternoon trimming the foresail. "I was transfixed by the sight of *FILA* as she slid down the waves. When her bow hit bottom, she threw up a huge cloud of spray and almost half the boat disappeared under the water. For a time I thought that the reason we're here on earth is to experience sights like that. You forget that your hands are frozen by the water temperature of three degrees Celsius (thirty-seven

Neil Hunter on *Palladin II*

degrees Fahrenheit) and the stress of the vibration and the fact that the autopilot cannot withstand the impact. The only important thing is that you're racing on the water."

Soldini, however, spent most of his time below where he had a small heater. Even then, it was cold, and when he typed on his computer, his fingers often froze and he would hit three keys instead of one.

One day while looking at a weather forecast on the Internet, he saw trouble. In six days, the fastest boats had covered more than 1,500 miles and were on a course that would take them south of the Kerguelen Islands, 2,000 miles north of Antarctica, midway between Africa and Australia. According to the forecast, a storm was spinning that way, too. South of the islands, the seabed rose from a depth of 13,000 feet to 900 feet. A storm could churn these relatively shallow waters into a deadly froth. Soldini beamed an e-mail to Autissier. She shared his concern. They watched the weather forecasts for a day. This was bad news. No one should go down there, they agreed. Autissier sent a message to Marc Thiercelin, while Soldini e-mailed Mike Golding in his rough English: "So wi don't take crezy risk. Are you agree??" Golding concurred and suggested a way point north of the islands. They contacted Josh Hall, who was struggling with a temperamental autopilot and had fallen behind the front-runners. All five agreed to stay north of the way point.

A steady westerly wind blew the five Finot boats across the icy Southern Ocean at a blinding pace. Thiercelin reported a top speed of thirty-eight knots (42 mph). The afternoon of December 13, Golding was helming through the swells, flying a three-sail rig, making a steady twenty-six knots. Suddenly, he realized that he was moving a little too fast and surfed over a wave. He felt as if he had driven over a cliff. The boat fell, the helm locked, and the rudder created a big rooster tail of spray as the boat's stern dug into the wave. Golding bent the tiller trying to keep control. The air filled with foam and water. He glanced at his speed: thirty knots and rising. He had a harness on, but it could snap. Fearing that he would be washed off the deck, he dove head-first into the cabin. A second later, the boat hit the bottom of the wave and a wall of water moving at about twenty knots washed over *Team Group 4's* wide deck. The mainsail made a nasty crunch as the boat jibed and fell on its side, and then . . . quiet.

My race is over, Golding thought, as he climbed onto the deck, now perpendicular to the sea.

Like Autissier, he had a swinging keel. He moved it to the center position. He also had some water ballast, and adjusted that. It was like playing a game of "Pickup Sticks." Do one thing at a time, and slowly the mess will sort itself out. He furled his genoa sail. Finally, after about a half hour of tweaking sails, the yacht began to come up, and he was off again.

One night, Josh Hall was surfing at twenty-seven knots, watching the water blast across the cabin windows. Winds were gusting to fifty knots, and the waves were at least thirty feet tall. This is getting hairy, Hall thought, and decided to pull down the mainsail. As the boat torpedoed through the darkness, he crawled forward and released the halyard, a line that hoists the mainsail. He looked out and saw a black ocean with white slashes where the waves were breaking. This is a raw night, he thought. He started crawling back to the cockpit, feeling his hands go numb from the cold. Suddenly, he felt the boat rise on a huge wave. He knew he was going to get nailed, and with a big hammer. He turned around and hugged the mast with all his strength as a torrent rushed over the deck. The water peeled him off the mast and threw him against the running backstay on the boat's stern. He wasn't clipped into his safety harness. If not for the backstay, he could have ended up in the water with his yacht sailing off at a twenty-five-knot clip.

Farther back in the pack, Brad Van Liew got out of his bunk one night to check the trim and start the engine to recharge his batteries when a huge wave crossed the boat and knocked it on its side. Van Liew was thrown across the cabin and his head hit the ballast control valve, knocking him unconscious. He woke up with a cut on his forehead and a big lump on his head. He had no idea how long he had been out.

A fierce gale damaged Neil Hunter's windvane steering device, which he had named "Mildred," prompting him to dive overboard to make a repair. "I have just put on my 7 mm wet suit and have been for a swim in the Southern Ocean," he said in a message. "I have sort of fixed Mildred but the balance is wrong and she needs at least 13 knots to hold a course. Will have a look at that today. Consequently George (his name for the autopilot) is back out there steering this morning."

Autissier's ride on the roller coaster also was taking its toll. On December 13, she sent a message to the ROC: "I am hanging in there and right now am doing better than 20 knots - while remaining constantly on the alert, ready to shorten sail." The weather was cold and gray. In another e-mail, she said: "Still no sun or if there is any, it's far behind the clouds, and since the heater is giving off black smoke, the interior is startling to look like a witch's den." On December 15, she wrote: "We really got knocked down this morning. The waves are starting to get a little vicious, running every which way, and one of them blind-sided the boat while I was brewing a cup of tea. Result: Mainsail and genoa hit the drink. No panic. Once the boat is lying on her side, nothing else happens. You have time to roller-furl the genoa, go get the backstay, shift the mainsail, and set off again . . . slowly."

A jibe is a difficult maneuver on a sailboat when sailing downwind. It happens when the wind shifts from one side to the other. Like a gust of wind turning a page of an open book, the sail flips from one side to the other. If not controlled, the boom slams violently across the boat. If a skipper's head happens to be in the way, the motion can cause serious injuries or death, and it can throw the unlucky skipper overboard. This quick shift of forces also can knock a boat on its side. Because Around Alone skippers were mostly sailing downwind in the Southern Ocean, and because they spent most of their time down below, uncontrolled jibes were a common occurrence and a constant source of problems.

During one jibe on *PRB*, the main sheet looped around the boat's satellite antenna and ripped it off. With the antenna gone, Autissier couldn't receive detailed weather forecasts, e-mails or her rivals' positions. This put her at a serious competitive disadvantage. Then, after two weeks at sea, midway between Australia and Antarctica, she noticed two screws on her sail track looked damaged. The sail track holds the sail tight to the mast. No big deal, she thought at first. Later, she jibed, and a six-inch piece of the mast track flew off about seven feet up the mast. More trouble. If she lowered the mainsail, she wouldn't be able to raise it again. But if a storm swept through, she might get blown over. The last weather forecast she had before her antenna blew off warned of 60-mph winds. She decided to head north, away from the heavier winds blowing below 50 degrees south latitude. Looking at the damage, she realized that she couldn't fix the mast herself. The nearest place with decent repair facilities was Hobart, Tasmania, several hundred miles to the north. She would have a difficult time winning the race now, she thought, as *PRB's* bow pointed toward Tasmania.

Meanwhile, in the Tasman Sea, a new storm was beginning to form.

A dismasted yacht founders during the Sydney-to-Hobart race.

A Deadly Storm

Christmas would be a busy time in the Tasman Sea. The leaders of the Around Alone were streaking in from the south while a large fleet of yachts was set to head south in the 54th annual Sydney-to-Hobart race.

Giovanni Soldini was the first Around Alone skipper to round the southern tip of Tasmania, sailing along the northern edge of a storm with 65-mph gusts. On Christmas Eve, he waited by the phone for his daughter, Martina, to call. Later, he had some Panettone, an Italian Christmas cake, and a glass of Spumante. It was a good holiday on *FILA*. On Christmas Day, he was more than 300 miles ahead of Mike Golding and 400 miles from Marc Thiercelin. Isabelle Autissier was on her way to Hobart, Tasmania for repairs and was no threat.

As if on cue, the skies cleared after twenty days of clouds. "A great Christmas present," Soldini said in a message to the ROC. He checked his e-mail and had nearly 200 Christmas greetings waiting to be read. Things were going well, but Soldini was keeping a sharp eye on a new storm brewing in the Tasman that could hit him head-on.

Hobart, a city of about 350,000, is the capital of Tasmania, a spade-shaped island that looks on maps as if it had broken off the southern tip of Australia. On this particular Christmas, Hobart was socked in with fog and rain. Autissier sailed toward Adventure Bay, south of the city. Waiting for her was a member of her shore team, Pierre-Jean Lemesle, and Phil and Robin Lee, the husband-and-wife shore crew for J.P. Mouligne.

Lee was a wide-shouldered, beer guzzling Australian with a thick handlebar mustache and long hair. In the 1994-95 BOC Challenge, Lee worked for David Adams, another Australian who took first place in the Class Two division. Lee was visiting his father in Sydney for Christmas when Adams telephoned: Autissier was headed to Hobart and needed help. Adams said he couldn't do anything because he was set to compete in the Sydney-to-Hobart race. He asked Phil if he would sort things out.

Putting their Christmas plans on hold, the Lees scrounged up some parts - no easy feat just before Christmas. "I walked into a hardware store while they were throwing a Christmas party," Lee recalled. "I said, You're not going to believe this story, but I need this and this and this,' and they said boy you can spin a good yarn' and gave me everything I needed." They booked a flight to Tasmania.

Autissier, meanwhile, was fighting headwinds and making slow progress. When the Lees, Lemesle and several other volunteers arrived in Adventure Bay on December 26, a group of reporters were waiting in a boat, getting drunk.

"What the hell are you guys doing down here," Lee asked.

"Waiting for Isabelle," they responded.

"Well, we're her support crew, stick with us guys," Lee said.

But as darkness fell, Autissier was still out there. The reporters gave up and went home. Three hours later, at about 4:00 a.m. on December 27, Autissier sailed into Adventure Bay. The night was ink black with fog and heavy rain. When Lee and Lemsle climbed aboard, Autissier smiled.

"So glad you're here," she said.

But she looked exhausted. She hadn't slept for two days. Once the boat was moored, Lee and Lemesle went to work. They divided the repairs: Lemesle would do the mast track, and Lee would fix the satellite antenna and hydraulic ram. When Lee opened the antenna package, he noticed that it didn't include a mounting bracket. He looked around and found a powdered milk can. Using the scissors on his Swiss Army knife, he cut the can so it looked like an octopus with its tentacles splayed about, and used it for a bracket. For five hours they worked in the rain. Autissier took a short nap, had a bite to eat and did some interviews. She was clearly frustrated by the turn of events.

"She was saying that she would be lucky to place in the race. She had written off winning," Lee said.

Despite the dreary weather and Autissier's disappointment, it was a playful and efficient crew that patched together *PRB*. While Lee held some bearings, Autissier walked up and said, "Phil, you have a lot of balls." Autissier and Lee's wife, Robin, stitched some tears on the mainsail. Autissier was a celebrity in Australia after her rescue in the 1994-95 race, and Lee mentioned a cartoon he saw in one of the local papers that showed two guys standing in Santa suits. One Santa said: "It's that time of year again." The other said: "Christmas?" The first one said, "No, it's when Isabelle Autissier comes around."

After ten hours, Autissier was ready to roll.

"You go girl," Lee said as she sailed out of Adventure Bay into what had become a deadly storm.

On Boxing Day, the day after Christmas, 115 yachts gathered in Sydney to compete in one of the oldest and largest off-shore sailing events, the Sydney-to-Hobart race. The race's 54th edition began on a cloudless day. More than 300,000 revelers packed the city's harbor to see off the huge fleet, which included the 79-foot *Sayonara*, owned by billionaire Larry Ellison, head of Oracle software. The course was 630 miles long and took the fleet through the Tasman Sea. The Tasman was known for its unpredictable conditions, especially in the shallow Bass Straits between Australia and Tasmania.

An hour and fourteen minutes after the 1:00 p.m. start, Australian meteorologists issued an updated forecast: A storm had developed. Packing 50- to 60-mph winds, it would churn up thirteen-foot seas. A few boats turned around, but most continued on. The barometer kept falling, the winds kept building. By the evening, some yachts were blasted by 90-mph gusts and thirty-foot seas. Nearly half the fleet sought shelter and quit the race. Others were caught in the storm or pushed on despite it. Seven boats had to be abandoned. Three sank. The Australian government launched a massive rescue with thirty-nine planes, six helicopters and three rescue boats. Fifty-five sailors were pulled from the thrashing seas with broken bones, hypothermia and other injuries. Only forty-nine boats made it to Hobart. British Olympic sailor Glyn Charles was swept off the deck of the *Sword of Orion* when it rolled 360 degrees, and his friends watched in horror as he tried to swim back. After twenty minutes, with the foundering yacht drifting away from Charles, the crew lost site of him in a distant wave. In all, six people died, the worst death toll in a sailing race since 1979 when fifteen people died in the British Fastnet race.

Soldini and the other Around Alone skippers were oblivious to the Sydney-to-Hobart disaster, but they were feeling the storm's fury. Soldini made sure he stayed away from the worst winds but the storm's tail hit him with 60-mph headwinds. He took down his mainsail. The waves were steep, and his boat did a miserable four knots. Soldini wasn't too worried, though. He had seen worse storms.

About 150 miles behind, Mike Golding also was in the storm, sailing through twenty-foot seas with 60-mph gusts. He logged onto his computer and started getting messages about the Sydney-to-Hobart fleet. Then he read about Glyn Charles washing overboard. The news hit like a sucker punch. He had sailed with Charles in the Admirals Cup a few years before. "It's a shock to find that someone you know has been killed in such a way," Golding said in a message to the ROC. "It brings home just how quickly things can go from control to chaos when racing in heavy weather - or at any time at sea for that matter."

As he sailed toward New Zealand, Soldini heard a quiet, *neek, neek, neek*. He knew every noise on his boat, and this one wasn't normal. He crawled out of the cabin and tracked it down. He went to the gooseneck, which holds the boom to the mast, and noticed that it was coming undone. He drilled into the fitting and fixed it with a screw. He had dodged a bullet. On December 29, he sent an e-mail: "Good news! My friend Mike is bogged down. There are almost 200 miles between us now, and I really think that I will have some wind until the 20th, and he won't - hopefully! I'm such a bad guy! Yesterday was really nice and crappy all around. Because of the news coming in from the Sydney-to-Hobart. It just got worse and worse. But also because sailing had made the news yet again because of a tragedy. Basically they only talk about this sport when someone is killed. And just to think that in Italy there are so many sailing fans, so many young kids who do it, we have the stuff of champions there. There are people who put their heart and souls into sailing and yet oftentimes they won't even give you two lines if you win. I remember well how it was at the beginning. But if a disaster happens, even if it's on the other side of the world, it's a different story. Ah well, what can you do. I'm off to my bunk now so goodnight."

A few days later, a member of his shore crew suggested they rent a helicopter to take a photo of him with the dramatic New Zealand mountains in the background. Soldini vetoed that idea. He was tired. It was a dangerous time in the race because of the coast's tricky currents and winds. Also, when he rounded Cape Reinga, the northern tip of New Zealand, the area gave him a funny feeling. He could feel the land's presence. The water's color looked dangerous. He sent a message to Autissier: Be careful, this place is no good.

On December 31, Soldini rounded the northern tip of New Zealand and sped south toward Auckland. "This hasn't been a great year for me - a lot of problems and pain. Let's hope things will be better in 1999," he said in a message.

At 4:24 a.m. on New Year's Day, after twenty-seven days and three hours at sea, he crossed the finish line for Leg Two. He had covered 6,884 miles at an average speed of eleven knots. A group of Maori dancers greeted him at the docks, and he fell into the arms of his wife, Elena. He held his daughter, Martina, who was fast asleep. "I'll stay awake as long as she does," Soldini said with a laugh and said it was one of the best days of his life.

"Winning after my terrible year has made me a happy man again," he told reporters. He talked about his friend's death, his disappointing finish during the first leg, and his critics. "They told me that I wasn't watching my opponents, that I was just going my own way, that I was wrong. It is difficult to understand the choices that are made at sea. But I was quite calm about it all. I have my own way of sailing. I follow the wind and sea and not my opponents. And that's how I'll always do it. This victory has proved me right and it's wonderful. I have re-established my relationship with the sea."

Things that go bump in the night

On New Year's Day, the same day Giovanni Soldini cruised into Auckland, Mike Golding rounded the northern tip of New Zealand. Golding wasn't worried about Soldini's victory in Leg Two. He knew that when he made it to Auckland, he would still be in first place overall, ahead of everyone by at least thirty-six hours. It was a solid lead. He felt rested and had a nice meal and a glass of wine for dinner. Life was good. He sat at the chart table and checked his position. He was supposed to veer toward the coast and rendezvous with a helicopter for some filming and publicity photographs. It would be a spectacular shot: A bright white *Team Group 4* flying along at fifteen knots with the beautiful amber New Zealand light bouncing off the waves, the mountainous coastline in the background. His main GPS system, which could pinpoint his location to a meter, was out though, and he had to use a less accurate system to chart his course. He also was missing a large-scale chart of the area, but a small-scale chart seemed sufficient. He sailed toward a spot about three miles off the coast. According to his interpretation of the charts, the area was clear and deep.

Golding had agreed to meet the helicopter at a predetermined point, and when he reached it, he could hear the helicopter's thwacking blades. Right on time. At least he knew he was plotting his course correctly. "That's amazing," the helicopter pilot told Golding about his clockwork navigation. Golding then steered *Team Group 4* toward the coast, and the filming began.

The seas here looked different, though. The waves were choppy, as if they were about to break. Must be because the two oceans meet north of the island, Golding thought. Maybe it was the tide. According to the charts, he was a mile from the nearest shallow water. No, something was wrong. He grabbed the helm. He looked at the depth finder. Only six feet under the keel! His speed: fifteen knots. Suddenly, he hit something. A grinding sound reverberated through the boat. He tried to steer out of the area.

Then the boat hit a second time, then a third. He cleared the shoal and went below.

Within a few minutes, *Team Group 4's* main compartment was ankle-deep in water.

Nine minutes after the collision, Golding radioed the New Zealand Coast Guard and explained what happened. He didn't request a mayday, but they issued one anyway. A nearby fishing boat, the *Happy One*, puttered out to see what was going on. The captain agreed to tow Golding's boat into a protected bay nearby. Golding then dialed Mark Schrader's cellular

Knee-deep in his flooded cabin, Golding waits to be towed to Auckland.

phone number.

Golding's voice was calm and steady, but Schrader immediately knew something was wrong. Golding said he had hit something on the north end of the island. He told Schrader his current position, explained that the keel looked damaged, and that water had flooded the main cabin.

Are you injured? Is the boat sinking? Schrader asked.

Golding said he was OK, and that the watertight bulkheads in the boat probably would keep the boat from sinking. His tone was matter-of-fact and concise, Schrader thought. Golding said he was more concerned that the keel might fall off.

"I'm not sure how badly damaged it is, but it looks bad," he told Schrader. He would have to wait until daylight to assess the damage. "I can't believed this happened."

He hung up and busied himself by trying to tidy up his boat. Could he have plotted the wrong course? What a lousy way to start the new year.

The next day, the boat's designer, Pascal Conq of Groupe Finot, motored out to Golding's yacht. Bad news, Conq said. The impact had nearly ripped off the keel. It could fall off at

any moment. There was extensive damage to the keel box, hydraulic rams and electronics. His engine had been flooded. The boat would have to be gently towed to Auckland and pulled out of the water to determine exactly what needed to be done. A tow longer than ten miles meant automatic disqualification.

Golding, sounding deflated and tired, phoned Schrader again and formally withdrew from the race.

On January 4, his boat was towed into Auckland. Golding was still on board, and when he crossed what would have been the finish line, it finally sank in: He was out of the race. All that time, all those plans, all that work. Over. Disqualified. He felt as if he had tripped twenty yards before the finish line in an Olympic race. He began to cry.

At a press conference later in the day, he accepted responsibility for the accident.

"Look," he told the reporters, "it was the stupidest thing I have ever done."

For weeks, Golding would have a tough time talking about the incident. He had never worked so hard in his life for something. Sure, he had started the race thinking it was just a tune-up for the Vendee Globe, but it had become so much more. He went over and over in his mind what happened.

True, had the helicopter not been there, he probably wouldn't have gone so close to the coast. That was a contributing factor. And he could have plotted the wrong course. But he had nailed the way point - the helicopter pilot had confirmed that - so his calculations had to be on the money. He looked at the video from the helicopter film crew; it too seemed to confirm his position on the charts. He studied the charts. They showed no sand bars.

The only thing that made sense was that the sand bar had moved.

Golding hung around the docks in Auckland, but it was an

awkward time. Midway through the race, the skippers and their shore crews had the kind of closeness soldiers feel when they've faced death. But he was no longer in the fight and felt like an outsider. "I have the feeling now," he said one afternoon while having a cappuccino at a nearby cafe, "that I'm a little bit of a leper. It's like when someone dies. They don't know what to say to you."

On January 1, two hours after Golding hit the sand bar, Marc Thiercelin's shore team reported that the Frenchman also had collided with something - probably a semi-submerged shipping container. The impact had damaged his rudders and forced him to stop for two hours to make repairs. He patched them together but was still having trouble steering.

Floating objects, particularly shipping containers, have become a serious problem. The standard twenty- and forty-foot metal boxes increasingly used in international trade sometimes fall off ships during storms and can float for days or longer depending on the cargo inside, bobbing in the waves like mines. Josh Hall and Neal Petersen had smashed into these before, with Hall losing his yacht in the last race. In addition to shipping containers, the ocean is littered with junk, driftwood and other boat killers. Soldini once hit a chunk of ice, destroying his rudder. In the Whitbread, a boat once collided with a pallet and then a plastic swimming pool. Whales were another danger.

With Golding out of commission and Thiercelin limping along, Isabelle Autissier stormed back into contention, making up the ground she lost with her damaged mast track and ten-hour diversion in Tasmania. When Thiercelin hit the container, she closed to within three-tenths of a mile.

Maybe, she hoped, she had left all her bad luck behind in the Indian Ocean.

Then, the morning she rounded the northern tip of New Zealand, sailing at about ten knots, she felt her boat collide

The fishing vessel *Happy One* tows an unhappy Golding across the Leg Three finish line in Auckland.

with something soft and big - big enough to stop a nine-ton boat in its tracks. Because the boat made a thud instead of a crack, she guessed it was a whale. And when she scanned the waves, there it was, a huge one swimming away. Then, she looked at her stern and saw that one of her two rudders was gone. So much for her quota of bad luck.

She had learned a lesson in the Vendee Globe when a broken rudder forced her into Cape Town for repairs - and out of the race. Now, she had a backup on board. She spent two hours putting it together and was off again. Thiercelin, however, was now seven miles ahead.

The two streaked south along New Zealand's emerald coast. As the sun set over the Hauraki Gulf, Thiercelin's golden boat *SOMEWHERE* sliced past the islands guarding Auckland's harbor and sailed toward Rangitoto, a dormant volcano near the finish line. He crossed after twenty-eight days and twenty-one hours at sea.

Autissier finished an hour later. Despite her pit stop and other problems, she was in first place overall, five hours ahead of Thiercelin and more than a day ahead of Soldini. "Incredible," she told a reporter.

Into New Zealand

CHAPTER FOURTEEN

For good luck, some sailors put a penny at the base of their boat's mast. J.P. Mouligne had a gold coin dating back to 1896. A friend, Wess Hoch, had worn it while fighting in Vietnam and believed it had saved his life. Hoch was chairman of North End Composites, a company in Rockland, Maine, that built the carbon fiber hull of *Cray Valley*. As the race wore on, Mouligne sometimes wondered if Hoch's coin was responsible for his good fortune.

Mouligne, the former knife thrower turned salesman turned ocean racer, had a smooth ride from Cape Town. His autopilots worked well. He had almost no damage. When the storm that devastated the Sydney-to-Hobart fleet passed by, the winds were in his favor and sent him flying through the Tasman Sea.

As dawn broke January 3, Mouligne glided over the finish line two days ahead of Mike Garside, his nearest rival in Class Two. He was just twelve hours behind Isabelle Autissier. Coming in so close to Autissier was an impressive achievement considering that his boat *Cray Valley* was only fifty feet long and carried 2,000 square feet of sail to Autissier's sixty-footer, which flew 3,000 square feet of cloth. He also beat Josh Hall by four days. Hall's sixty-foot *Gartmore Investment Management* had been pegged as the fastest boat in the race.

Still at sea, Garside conceded that Mouligne was in a league of his own. "I am totally impressed," the crusty Brit said in a message to the ROC. "For pity's sake, will some sponsor please give him a new 60 in time for the Vendee or the next Around Alone? He is so focused and good at this game, I have no doubt he is more than ready to take on - and beat - the world's best solo 60s sailors, now."

Garside's trip across the Southern Ocean, meanwhile, did nothing to improve his opinion about sailing. The water was dark and gray. His autopilot was on the fritz. The Sydney-to-Hobart storm spun by him on its way toward Antarctica and sucked all the wind out of the Tasman Sea. For days, his yacht plodded along at three or four knots. On January 9, as he passed the northern tip of New Zealand, he told the ROC, "I can sit here at my nav station and honestly say that the last 11 days of this race have been one of the most dreary, depressing experiences of my life. I have spent the endless days and nights creeping forward to my Auckland destination at the pace of a half-dead snail. I have despaired as the yachts ahead of me sped over the horizon with all the winds they needed. I have agonized as the yachts behind me closed up even more quickly. They arrived on a breeze that mocks me . . . I will never be able to look back on the Tasman Sea with any pleassure at all."

When Brad Van Liew rounded the southern tip of Australia and entered the Tasman Sea, he was more than 450 miles behind Garside. Determined to catch up, Van Liew spent hour after hour on deck, hoisting spinnakers, pulling jibs, jibing and tacking, trying to gain every inch. It was the most exhausting exercise Van Liew had ever done, mind-blowing in its repetition. He skipped meals. One day he worked twenty-two hours straight, averaging a measly three knots. On January 5, he sent a message to the ROC: "Mike and I have now shared something so profound and agonizing that I think that we might have to be blood brothers or married or some crazy thing. I would think our bond is as great as if we had been in battle together! My brain and body want to shut down so badly."

By January 9, Van Liew had made up the 450 miles. As dusk fell, Garside spotted Van Liew's navigation lights behind him. A few hours later, the lights seemed to vanish and Garside wondered if the American had turned them off, technically a violation of international maritime rules.

Unknown to Garside, Van Liew was playing games with his lights. He had two sets, one on the deck and another on the top of his mast. Every time he tacked, he switched the light configuration. One time he turned on only his tiny mast light so his boat would seem far off and small. After another turn, he switched on his floodlights to make his boat look huge. "He didn't know where I was," Van Liew would say later. "But I was right there all the time. I like to mess with him."

When the sun rose, the winds picked up, and the two screamed south toward Auckland. At one point, Garside watched Van Liew head for a cliff. For a split second, he thought, 'that will solve my problems.' Then he thought, 'maybe he's asleep.' He raised Van Liew on the VHF.

"Brad, are you awake? You're not sailing into that cliff, are you?"

"I'm OK. Thanks for the heads-up anyway."

Van Liew used the wind effect from the cliff to sail around the island, a maneuver that put him ahead for a short time. Soon, the two were sailing just a few feet apart, flying at between fifteen and twenty knots with a stiff thirty-knot wind blowing across their bows. They were so close they could talk with each other, though the noise from the wind and waves made it difficult to hear exactly what they were saying.

Garside thought he heard Van Liew suggest they sail in at the same time. They had joked in the past about rafting their boats together. Then he heard Van Liew shout. "That's the worst reef I've ever done."

Garside didn't know what he was talking about.

"Can you see the finish line!" Van Liew shouted.

"No!" Garside yelled back.

Garside had no idea where the line was; he didn't expect to sail so fast down the coast and hadn't had time to check his charts. Then he recognized the volcano. He remembered the line was somewhere near it. Slowly, with each wave, Garside started pulling ahead. Garside sped over the line after thirty-five days and seventeen hours at sea. Van Liew followed two minutes and twenty-one seconds later, the closest finish in the race's history.

Days later, Garside still wondered why Van Liew seemed to slow down at the end. "He swears he didn't, but I still think he gave the leg to me."

Just seven hours after the Garside-Van Liew duel, Viktor Yazykov crossed the finish line. He was in terrific spirits. Unlike the first leg, in which he battled a dangerous episode of depression and had to slice open an abscess on his elbow, his voyage across the Southern Ocean was relatively uneventful. His most significant problem happened midway when his satellite communications equipment failed. During the first leg he thought all the communication requirements cheapened the singlehanded experience. But over time, he grew to depend on the messages, weather faxes and other information, and when his satellite link went down, it took him a few days to get used to the quiet.

Alone, though, he felt even closer to his boat. He talked to it nonstop. Sometimes it seemed to talk back. When surfing down a wave, it made a loud *wooooooo*, almost like a car engine. When something went wrong, he would ask the boat for an answer. Early on, his asymmetrical spinnaker got caught in his genoa, a potentially serious problem. If winds picked up, the big, flapping spinnaker could pull the boat over. "What do you want, asymmetrical spinnaker?" he asked the sail. "What should I do? Would you like something?" Then he came up with an idea. He crawled onto the foredeck and in the rolling seas, he twisted the spinnaker around the forestay. "It wasn't easy, but when I was done, I could believe I solved the problem."

Without e-mails and position reports, he had no idea where the other boats were. So he focused on racing the boat as best he could, figuring everyone else was way ahead. But as he rounded the southern tip of Australia, he was just behind Brad Van Liew, an impressive performance for a forty-foot boat. Van Liew had set his sights on Garside, though, and pulled away. When he made it into Auckland, someone told him that Garside and Van Liew had come in earlier in the day. "Really? I did not know anything," he replied. "That's incredible. I would never have expected that. I just wanted to finish as quick as possible." He was bursting with pride over his boat, his gold tooth showing when he smiled. "It was such an unbelievable feeling. You would be with huge waves, and there would be small waves on them, and you would go down these waves so fast and straight. You felt like you were part of the wave. Beautiful."

On January 27, Minoru Saito, who turned sixty-five during the leg, drifted into Auckland. It was a broiling afternoon with no wind, and Saito floated like a piece of driftwood across the line. When race director Mark Schrader climbed on board, the smell almost knocked him overboard. Schrader hesitated to

Minoro Saito arrives in Auckland

ask Saito about the odor, but then Saito said. "Boat stink very bad." He explained that midway in the leg, his alternator broke, cutting power to a refrigerator full of pork, chicken, beef and fish heads. Over time his groceries began to rot. "I don't want to open the lid," he said, opening his mouth and sticking out his tongue in a grimace. At the docks, New Zealand agricultural inspectors wearing rubber gloves hauled off the food in large plastic bags.

That evening, as the twilight turned Auckland's harbor a soft amber, Neal Petersen sped across the line. "What took you so long?" Petersen's girlfriend Gwen Wilkinson shouted from a chase boat. When he was towed to the docks, the South African national anthem blared from a loudspeaker. Viktor Yazykov gave Petersen a bear hug. Race organizers handed him a plate of sushi and between gulps, he told Gwen and others milling around the docks that the voyage had been the toughest experience of his life. Soon after leaving Cape Town, he developed a case of "trench foot," a condition common among front-line soldiers in World War I. For about three weeks, he could barely feel his feet, which made it dangerous to move around the deck. During one storm, winds knocked

Fedor Konioukhov on *Modern University for the Humanities*

over his yacht six times in five hours. As he neared New Zealand, while taking a nap, his boat hit something heavy and hard. He listened to it as it bounced along his hull. He never saw what he hit but from the sharp sound it made against the hull, he figured it was a floating oil drum or pallet. The collision put a hole in the bow, and the boat began to leak. For a split second, he thought his race was over. But it turned out to be a minor leak and he continued on. When he made it to Auckland, he felt a sense of satisfaction but already was thinking about the leg ahead. "I won't feel good until I make it around Cape Horn." Still, he was happy about his performance. "A lot of people were concerned in Charleston about the seaworthiness of the boat, and there were rumors that they weren't going to let me race," he said. "But my boat is here." Brad Van Liew, who had bet that Petersen wouldn't make it to Auckland, would still be irked by Petersen's speeches during the stop in Auckland but had to admit that he was impressed with his performance. "You know, this is not easy what we're doing. So I've got to hand it to him. He sailed that boat halfway around the world."

When Fedor Konioukhov was fifteen, he sailed a small wooden boat across the Sea of Azov alone. When he made it back, his father, a military man, beat him and destroyed the boat, saying "no more adventures." As teens are wont to do, Konioukhov ignored those orders, and his life has since been filled with one adventure after another. As a young man, he fought in Vietnam with the North Vietnamese. Then as the Cold War thawed, he climbed the highest mountains in the world, trekked to the poles and sailed twice around the world on his own. "He is a complicated man. All you have to do is look in his eyes," his son, Oscar, said one afternoon in Auckland. "You can never tell Fedor what to do. There are too many rules in the race, and he's a rule breaker. But only a man like that can climb Mount Everest and sail around the world." At the time, Oscar was waiting for his father to call Mark Schrader and discuss his future in the race. "Fedor is not satisfied with how he has done. He told me that he has reached his limit. He has run out of luck, and he is, how do you say, out of gut power. Every man has a limit, and he has reached his."

Race rules required all the skippers to be in a week before the restart, and Konioukhov was expected to miss the deadline by a few days. The rule was designed to keep the fleet together as much as possible throughout the race. The 4,000-mile void between New Zealand and Cape Horn was a lonely and dangerous place. Roughly midway was a point that was the farthest place on the planet you could be from land. Only a handful of ships plied these waters. A few renegade fishing fleets also operated illegally in the area but couldn't be counted on for any help. Rescue options were limited mainly to the other skippers. The fleet was its own safety net, and if the net's holes got too large, a skipper starting late or lagging too far behind might fall through.

As he had done after the start in Charleston, Konioukhov baffled race officials after leaving Cape Town by taking an odd route toward New Zealand. For the first week, while battling a bad flu, he zig-zagged his way around the tip of Africa. One day he sailed in the opposite direction. "Please don't think that I am going for Madagascar. I am heading towards Auckland," he told the ROC in one message and then gave race officials a detailed description of a cocktail he used to ward off the cold.

The ingredients included rum, pepper, spices, vodka and red wine. "After this cocktail I can be on a deck for a long time. There is one shortcoming - once upon a time after this rough cocktail, I find that I was sailing wrong directions."

Later, his generators failed. Because skies were so dark and gray, he couldn't juice up his communications equipment and his autopilot. Then, he sailed far south until he saw chunks of ice floating in the water. According to race rules, skippers were supposed to stay north of a way point about 1,000 miles south of Australia, a rule designed to make sure the fleet was within range of Australian rescue teams. But Konioukhov's faulty ballast system and a strong southerly wind pushed him too far south to make the way point. He missed it by thirty miles. Now, with the deadline to be in Auckland about to pass, Konioukhov was set to break another race rule.

Mark Schrader had mixed emotions about Koniouhkov. He admired his courage and was awed by his accomplishments, but he was clearly irked by the Russian's lack of communication and wasn't sure about his skills as a sailor. As the deadline loomed, he received e-mails from across Russia pleading for leniency. He couldn't read many of them because they were in Russian, but he got the gist from the few English phrases he could pick out. "He's an icon up there," Schrader said, rubbing his eyes one afternoon. But the rules were the rules. Schrader didn't want any skipper leaving late this time. When the deadline passed, Konioukhov was still several hundred miles away.

Before race officials had a chance to discuss Konioukhov's status, the Russian beat them to the punch. In a message to Schrader, Konioukhov said: "Today is the deadline for arriving in Auckland, and I am still several days from completing Leg Two of Around Alone. I have encountered many technical difficulties with my boat since the beginning of the race and those problems have worsened in the Southern Ocean. I know now that the difficulties that I am experiencing with my boat do not allow me to continue on within the boundaries of the race. Therefore I think it best for me to retire officially from

Around Alone and then find a way to continue my personal quest and meet my commitments to my partner in Moscow, Modern University."

~~~

When the deadline passed, Konioukhov wasn't the only skipper still trying to make it in. Robin Davie was even farther behind - more than a week away from Auckland. His situation was even more perplexing than the Russian's. On December 5, when the fleet left Cape Town, Davie told people on the docks that he would leave a day or two after the fleet. He explained that he simply had too much work to do on his boat and didn't want to risk taking an unprepared vessel into the Southern Ocean. This made sense to Schrader, who appreciated Davie's caution. But Davie didn't shove off for ten days. When he finally did make it onto the water, his new rudder didn't seem tuned to his boat. When South Carolina reached certain speeds, the boat went out of control and he had to slow down. He was stuck in low winds for several days. Then his forestay snapped, threatening the integrity of his mast, and slowing him even more. He sent a message to race officials asking them to take his problems into account. (Davie was unaware at the time but one of his supposedly watertight bulkheads had flooded, adding an extra ton of weight to his boat, slowing it even more.). Schrader knew Davie well. He respected Davie's knowledge and skills as a seagoing handyman. But in Cape Town he had taken Davie aside and told him that he wouldn't let him leave late in Auckland. He was against Davie continuing. "Why have rules then?" After convening a committee of race officials, organizers disqualified Davie.

Halfway through the race, only twelve out of the original sixteen were still in the hunt.

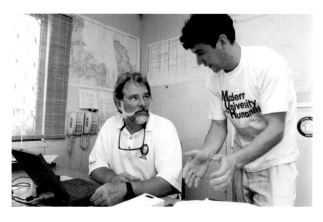

Oscar Konioukhov discusses his father's status in the race with Around Alone Director Mark Schrader.

Marina in downtown Auckland

INTO THE WIND

Around Together

It was the first time that the Around Alone had stopped in Auckland. In the previous four races, Sydney had been the host. But after the 1994-95 race, organizers felt the event got lost in that big city, and Auckland was eager to take Sydney's place. Auckland is a comfortable city. Its 1.3 million residents make up one-third of the country's population. With its rolling hills, coffee shops and leafy suburbs, it resembles Seattle. It even has its own version of the Space Needle.

Known as the "City of Sails," Auckland has one of the most robust yachting communities in the world. Massive marinas with dense forests of masts spill into the harbor. When Team New Zealand won the America's Cup in 1995, it shocked the international yachting community, but not folks in New Zealand. Sailing is serious business there. One out of every six residents in Auckland owns a boat, the highest per capita of any major city in the world. On any afternoon when the weather is nice, the blue-green waters of the city's harbor are awash in sailboats challenging each other in regattas.

Team New Zealand's victory meant the Kiwis would stage the next contest, which promised to be an elaborate and expensive affair. First a challenger had to be selected, and sixteen syndicates from around the world shelled out a non-refund-able entry fee of $250,000. (The entry fee for the Around Alone is $12,500.) These syndicates would fight it out in late 1999 with the winner taking on New Zealand's boat in 2000.

By the time the Around Alone fleet arrived in Auckland, Team New Zealand and the challenging syndicates already had built large warehouses along a pier in the New Zealand Cup Village, a new waterfront development in the heart of the city's downtown. These sheds were the size of airplane hangars. The yachts themselves rested in cradles, their towering twelve-story masts matching the top floors of some of the city's hotels. City leaders predicted these syndicates would spend as much as $400 million on new boats, parts, housing and other services. It would be by far the most expensive yacht race the world had ever seen.

The Around Alone clearly was a sideshow to the America's Cup. "We're just a warm-up," Mark Schrader said one morning. But Schrader and other race officials were pleased with the facilities and the throngs of visitors who ambled through the piers to get a glimpse of the Around Alone fleet. "There are good sailors everywhere," Schrader said, "But I can't think of another place where there are so many knowledgeable people and such good facilities concentrated in one place."

The Around Alone yachts were stationed on an island in a

Robin Lee works on mast of *Cray Valley*

basin across from the syndicate warehouses. One warm, gray morning, J.P. Mouligne and his shore crew removed the mast from *Cray Valley* to do some repairs. Without its mast, *Cray Valley* looked especially wide and flat, like an upside down iron. They moved the boat across the canal to an area borrowed from one of the Cup syndicates. Below the bright yellow Swiss entry, five masts from the Around Alone yachts were on the ground in rows, like fallen timber. Mouligne's shore team, Phil and Robin Lee, worked side-by-side with the shore crews for Isabelle Autissier and Giovanni Soldini.

Standing in the shadows of the America's Cup boats, Mouligne said he couldn't believe how much money was being poured into that race. "They won't say exactly how much they spend, because they're all very secretive, but the number you hear is sixty million dollars. Incredible," he said.

"The Around Alone and America's Cup are so different," he continued. "Our boats are faster and stronger. You don't need twelve people to sail our boats. Those boats are very fragile. They can't sail in chop or when the wind is over twenty knots. They will never sail across the Atlantic. And the spirit of the race is completely different. They are very secretive and high on themselves. Here, we are all friends. Everyone helps each other. There's a real sense of comradeship. We want to beat each other in the race, of course, but we also know that our lives depend on the guy who might be behind you. We all go drink together. Isabelle is a national hero in France, but you would never think that. She's totally normal. Very approachable. Same with Giovanni. He's a kind of happy-go-lucky guy. But the America's Cup has earned a reputation for stuffiness. I think that's really bad in the sport because yachting is still perceived as an elite type of sport. The blue blood, blue-blazer New York Yacht Club attitude has done us a lot of damage. On the other hand, singlehanded sailing has a way of making you humble. When you're out there alone, you face yourself. You make mistakes, sometimes you get seasick. You look in the mirror, and you look like a freak. You don't put on a show for someone. You feel a deep sense of accomplishment but you also feel small and lucky to be alive."

After working hard on the boats all day, the Around Alone skippers and shore crews convened at the Viaduct Central, the nearest tavern, where they often worked just as hard on their bar tabs. In a sense, the race's name was misleading. The skippers sailed alone around the world, but they did so together. The race was an eight-month exercise in international group dynamics. When the fleet left Charleston, nine countries were represented. Some skippers were old friends, others were strangers to the singlehanded sailing circuit. As they sailed together, they created an experience unique to the group, a bond that was difficult to describe to outsiders.

"There is no other fraternity like this," Brad Van Liew said one afternoon on the docks. Van Liew and Josh Hall, for instance, had become especially close, eating dinner and partying until sunup. "I know that if he got in trouble, I would risk my life to help him, and he would do the same for me."

The bonds between the skippers were fairly thin from Charleston to Cape Town, but grew stronger in Cape Town. It was during the stopovers where the skippers could talk about their experiences on the water, like soldiers on leave. This social aspect was one reason why Giovanni Soldini preferred the

Around Alone over the nonstop Vendee Globe. "I like this race because it's a big family with a big history." In the Vendee, Isabelle Autissier added, she and Marc Thiercelin raced together but never had the chance to get to know each other. "Sometimes you arrive fifteen days apart."

As happens in many large groups, cliques often develop, and some people are more popular than others. The amiable Van Liew often was a ringleader at gatherings, encouraging as many parties as he could. At the other end of the spectrum was Marc Thiercelin.

Thiercelin was rarely seen on the docks or at parties. He sometimes missed supposedly mandatory race functions. One night when Thiercelin walked by on the docks, Neal Petersen smiled and said, "The mystery man." Another night after a little wine, Van Liew and Hall half-joked with Thiercelin's shore team manager that *SOMEWHERE* ought to be renamed *SOMEWHERE ELSE.* "Where is your guy? You know he's taking a lot of crap," Van Liew told him. Later, Van Liew would say with a sneer, "he only cares about the next Vendee."

A former cabinet maker and advertising artist, Thiercelin was a compact and handsome man who was voted "most sexy guy" in the last Vendee Globe. He created a sailing school in France for children and a board game called "Captain Marck," which he sold to raise money for the Vendee. He had placed second in the race after Christophe Auguin and had become a well-known sailing figure in his country.

Unlike the affable Mouligne or Van Liew, who were comfortable with reporters, Thiercelin was a public relations challenge. His English was limited, and he was uncomfortable doing interviews with the mostly English-speaking reporters covering the race. That and his shyness gave him an aura of arrogance and aloofness. One-on-one, though, he was a thoughtful man who had a deep passion for sailing and the sea. "My sponsor sometimes puts pressure on me to do interviews, but I try to stay quiet with the media. And when I am in the race, I am in the race, but when I am not in the race, I have my own

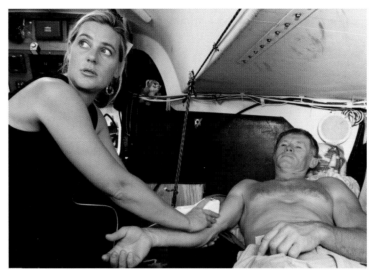

life. I leave the boat with my crew, which I have confidence in. But I prefer to stay quiet."

In Auckland, though, it was difficult for the skippers to avoid the spotlight. A week before the restart, the skippers were taken to a massive concert in a city park. During the event, four giant construction cranes danced to *Swan Lake*, eventually hatching a baby crane. The crowd went wild. When the skippers were asked to walk on stage, the crowd of 150,000 rose to their feet again. While waiting to go on stage, Mike Garside and Isabelle Autissier chatted. "She told me that the Southern Ocean was not her friend. She said this is the last time, my number's up.' I couldn't believe it."

During the last days before the restart, the skippers gathered to discuss safety issues and the weather. During this leg, the fleet would dive deep into the Southern Ocean toward Antarctica. In one briefing, Mark Schrader urged the skippers to report any ice they saw. "Remember there are people coming behind you."

Leg Three was the most daunting of the race's four parts,

Left: Oxana Makhno uses magnetic laser therapy to help Viktor Yazkov recuperate. Above: Giovanni Soldini.

Autissier and Hall prepare for Leg Three

"four thousand miles of the most difficult sailing you'll ever do," Schrader said. It had the same powerful westerly winds and strong currents as the second leg, but Leg Three had Cape Horn.

Cape Horn was the symbolic summit of the race. Skippers sometimes described it as the Everest of sailing. It is the closest land to the Antarctic ice pack. It's also where the Atlantic and Pacific oceans meet. It is a giant funnel, with the tip of South America dipping toward the Antarctica Peninsula, which juts north and looks on maps like the handle of a frying pan. Into this funnel goes the Southern Ocean's wind and currents. Scientists estimated that one current moves 140 million cubic feet of water per second by Cape Horn - 5,000 times as much as the Amazon River. Winds rush down the Andes and collide with the westerly winds, making the seas unpredictable and steep. The area is littered with shipwrecks.

For some like Neal Petersen and Viktor Yazykov, rounding the cape meant the fulfillment of a lifelong dream. For others, it was a symbol of relief. "When you pass Cape Horn, you go back into the South Atlantic and you feel like you're going back home," Giovanni Soldini said. Autissier added: "Cape Horn means the end of big troubles - no more freezing cold and no more huge waves and heavy winds." Autissier had been past the cape four times. "When you leave the Southern Ocean it's a big relief, but then you start to miss it because it's such a special place. So this will be my fifth time - I hope."

The morning of the restart, February 6, a troop of Maoris, native New Zealanders, performed a ceremony on the docks to scare away the evil spirits. Minoru Saito vowed to sail to the location where Harry Mitchell was lost. "Harry I will say, I give you the gold earring. Then I throw it into the sea."

The harbor was a mass of sails as more than 300 spectator boats waited for Sir Edmund Hillary, the famous mountaineer and a New Zealand native, to fire the starting gun. Petersen was over the line first and, as usual, was quickly passed by the bulk of the fleet. As usual, Autissier stayed back. With fifteen knots of wind filling their sails, the fleet sailed off on what would become the race's most traumatic leg.

Dismasted

CHAPTER SIXTEEN

The little plane flew low over the water, orbiting *FILA* in the fading New Zealand sunlight.

Giovanni Soldini immediately recognized the airplane, a two-seater Falco. He had flown it just the week before. Its pilot was Luciano Nustrini, a seventy-year-old Italian expatriate living in Auckland. Nustrini was a retired airport architect who had moved to New Zealand to teach. Now and then, he earned a little extra income writing about sailing. Soldini had met him a few years earlier at a cocktail party in Italy. Nustrini also was a sailor and had a son named Giovanni. The two became friends, and after Soldini arrived in Auckland, Nustrini offered to teach him to fly.

As Nustrini buzzed by, Soldini figured he was just trying to get a few more photographs of the boat. The fleet was only a few hours into Leg Three, still well within range of the media's eye. But even with his limited flight experience, Soldini could tell something was wrong. The airplane wasn't flying as smoothly as it did when he and Nustrini flew over the America's Cup boats in Auckland Harbor the week before.

Suddenly, as the plane turned, it began to fall. Belly-up, it crashed into the Hauraki Gulf.

The plane hit the water a quarter-mile off the bow of Brad Van Liew's *Balance Bar*, the only other boat in the area. Soldi-ni was in *FILA*'s cockpit when he saw the crash. He dove into the cabin, reaching for the VHF radio on his navigation table.

"Mayday, mayday," Soldini called over the radio. "An airplane has crashed into the water."

Aboard *Balance Bar*, Van Liew heard his radio squawk to life.

"Brad, it crashed right in front of you. You're about to hit it!" Soldini said.

Van Liew had seen the plane circling overhead and paid little attention to it. He had just ducked inside the cabin to check a navigation chart. When he went back on deck, Van Liew hadn't noticed the plane was gone, but he smelled the sickening odor of aviation fuel.

Van Liew didn't see any wreckage. The plane carrying Nustrini and his wife, Giuliana, had disappeared in 150 feet of water. He called the New Zealand Coast Guard and reported his position. They told him to stand by. They would send boats and a helicopter. As he tacked, Van Liew scanned the water for survivors.

Van Liew got back on the radio. "Did you see the crash?" he asked Soldini. "What position was the plane in when it hit the water?" Soldini replied that the plane had flipped as it started to turn and hit the water upside down.

A professional pilot, Van Liew knew an inverted crash was bad news. "If the aircraft was inverted at the time of the crash, there's no way anybody survived that," he would say later. "Nobody ever has, nobody ever will."

As much as he would have liked to find survivors, Van Liew was sure that wouldn't happen. He asked the Coast Guard if they needed him for anything, then asked if he could go. They thanked him for his time and sent him on his way.

Before the crash, Van Liew was optimistic about his chances on the third leg. In upwind conditions, *Balance Bar* had an advantage over the Finots piloted by his Class Two competitors, J.P. Mouligne and Mike Garside. He was trying to open up as big a lead as possible before turning at New Zealand's East Cape and dipping back into the Southern Ocean. The crash cast a pallor over his trip, and now he didn't feel much like racing.

Van Liew and Soldini sailed side-by-side through the night. Over their VHF radios, the two skippers talked for an hour about Nustrini. Soldini was upset. He had lost yet another friend. "Luciano was a great person, and to see his plane fall out of the sky was a nightmare," Soldini said in an e-mail to the ROC.

As the two skippers rounded East Cape and steered into the Southern Pacific, their conversation turned to families and sailing. It helped a little to talk, but Van Liew's spirits were low.

A few days later, Van Liew still led the small-boat division, but Mouligne and Garside were within a few nautical miles. Van Liew checked his computer and had an e-mail message from Josh Hall. Van Liew and Hall had become great friends at the race stopovers in Auckland and Cape Town, closing down bars together. They saw each other as brothers of a sort, each the underdog of his division in the Around Alone. Through e-mails and over the radio, they talked several times a day. They used call signs taken from the movie *Top Gun*, which Hall

watched on a DVD player aboard his yacht. Hall was Maverick, Van Liew the Iceman.

But the message on Van Liew's laptop this morning contained none of their usual collegial banter.

"Brad, mast is overboard. I'm cutting it loose, sorting it out. More later. Josh."

Van Liew was dumbstruck. As he swung *Balance Bar* around on an intercept course, he thought: What next?

Things had been looking up for Hall since the Leg Three restart. After a fourth-place finish on the first leg and a fifth-place finish on the second, he felt as if his boat finally was living up to its potential. Many of the skippers considered the colorful *Gartmore Investment Management* to be the fastest yacht in the fleet, and Hall shared their opinion. His goal was to be the first boat around Cape Horn, and the morning of February 11, he was within a few miles of the race leaders.

Thirty-five knots of wind pushed his boat through heavy seas, and Hall had everything battened down, three reefs in his mainsail. With the wind coming from just forward of the beam, spray soaked the deck as *Gartmore*'s hull slammed into the waves. Hall felt comfortable with the boat's motion, though. Nursing the flu, he had little to do but sit back and enjoy the ride. "The boat just eats that stuff up," he had said in an e-mail to race headquarters the day before.

And then, ka-bang. The noise sounded like a shotgun in his ear. The bang was soon followed by a crash.

Hall was at the chart table in his cabin, plotting his position. He looked out the window in time to see his ninety-foot mast tumble overboard. It broke off just under the lower spreaders. Hall dashed out of the cabin. With a grinder, he began to cut away the rigging. He managed to salvage the mainsail, which had been triple-reefed to the boom, but he had to saw off the mast. Hanging over the side, it could knock a hole in the boat's hull and flood the cabin.

Giovanni Soldini and Brad Van Liew on the docks in Auckland

After wrestling with the mast for more than an hour, Hall winched the rig onto *Gartmore*'s foredeck but saw little to save. It looked like a carbon fiber junk heap. He threw it overboard.

Hall was 800 miles east of New Zealand when his boat was dismasted. The nearest land was the Chatham Island chain 300 miles back. Hall reasoned that he could make the Chathams in a few days, but he was too tired to set up a jury rig now. He fired off the message to Van Liew, the closest skipper to his position, and one to race headquarters.

Van Liew had already diverted by the time race officials ordered him to turn toward Hall. The irony of it escaped no one. Van Liew's boat, *Balance Bar*, was skippered in the 1994-95 race by Alan Nebauer under the name *Newcastle Australia*. Early in that race, Hall's boat struck something in the Atlantic, probably a shipping container, and began to sink. It was Nebauer and *Newcastle* who rescued Hall off a deck awash in ocean water on a black South Atlantic night.

Now, it appeared Hall was out of another Around Alone race, and the same boat was on course to rescue him.

After a few hours' rest, Hall had a fresh look at the situation and told Van Liew to continue racing. He fashioned a jury rig with his spinnaker pole and staysail and broke the race seal on his engine. Motor-sailing, Hall chugged toward the Chathams at a miserable three knots. In a message to Claire Lewis, a member of his shore crew in England, Hall said he was devastated.

"We were finally in strong conditions with working pilots and a great new sail, and I was pacing the others well," he said. "I really felt the second half of the race could be ours, and in one second we have nothing. So much effort and time and money, and still we get stuffed."

It didn't make sense. *Gartmore*'s mast had been pulled in Auckland, and the whole boat had been given a thorough inspection. The mast had not been torn from the boat in a knockdown; it simply broke off at deck-level in normal conditions for Finot yachts. Hall and his shore crew suspected some kind of defect with the carbon fiber mast, but they would never know. The evidence was now at the bottom of the sea.

As the reality of his situation set in, Hall let off steam in an e-mail to Van Liew.

"Talk about deja vu, me in trouble and once again your boat being the closest. Remind me never to go racing without that machine in the fleet. Don't know if I'm angry, disappointed, depressed or what. All those things and more I guess. I'll never have such a good machine or program going and still it happens. Why doesn't this ever happen to Christophe Auguin? You're sailing for both of us now. Give 'em hell."

Puttering toward the Chathams, Josh Hall officially withdrew from the Around Alone. Now, only ten boats were left in the fleet, just three sixty-footers.

Most of the skippers were deeply affected by Hall's fate. Van Liew started looking skyward at his mast more often. Mike Garside also was nervous. His mast was made by the same people who made Hall's. Isabelle Autissier noted in an e-mail to race headquarters, "Division one is shrinking to the size of a handkerchief."

Gartmore under sail

Isabelle Autissier at the tiller of *PRB*

Capsized!

CHAPTER SEVENTEEN

Pushed by 30-mph winds, *PRB* streaked toward Cape Horn at a lightning pace of 375 miles a day. In the ten days since Leg Three began, Isabelle Autissier had traveled halfway across the empty stretch of water between New Zealand and South America. Surfing down thirty-foot waves, *PRB* often cut through the froth heeled over on its ear.

She let the autopilot steer and ventured out of the cabin only once or twice a day to adjust sails. She flew as much canvas as *PRB* could hold in the weather, trying to keep pace with Marc Thiercelin. She took short naps between study sessions with her charts and weather forecasts from her computer. Sometimes she looked out the window, trying to catch a glimpse of sunlight breaking through the clouds and lighting the wind-streaked seas. Squalls kept knocking the boat off course, so she had to keep an eye on her heading.

"In the gusts, the boat shoots off pretty brutally," she said in a message to the ROC on February 13. "A little while ago, I was knocked off the chart table bench and landed on my head."

Autissier was in a good mood. It seemed as if she had finally put her Southern Ocean troubles behind her. She had fixed her mast track problems and now, after Golding's crash, led the race. With her boat cruising through the water like a torpe-do, she felt her confidence grow. She plunged farther and farther south, trying to cut the miles she would have to travel.

Because the planet is a sphere, the shortest distance between two points is never the straight line it appears to be on most maps. The shortest route is always a curved line. In nautical terms, this is called the rhumb line or a great circle route. The rhumb line between New Zealand and South America cuts deep into the seas swirling around Antarctica. It was tempting for sailors to shave off miles by sailing below 50 degrees, or even 60 degrees, south latitude. But doing so was risky because of icebergs and smaller chunks of ice called growlers. Race rules prohibited dropping too close to Antarctica, where icebergs are the size of islands and can snap carbon fiber boats like toothpicks. Autissier was sailing at 55 degrees south, closer to Antarctica than most skippers would dare. She wasn't alone, though. About 100 miles ahead, Marc Thiercelin had dipped just as far south.

Giovanni Soldini, meanwhile, took a more conservative northerly route, sailing against his reputation as a gambler. He wanted to avoid a low pressure system spinning across 55 degrees south latitude. The way Soldini saw it, his course would pay dividends later. Thiercelin and Autissier would get plastered by a storm, and he could skirt around it, using its wind

Autissier at *PRB*'s nav station

other low, probably a more powerful one," she said in a message to the ROC. "It's getting really cold, and the seas are pretty large, but things are all right. Lots of time spent on watch; not much new happening."

On February 15, a rare burst of sunshine broke through the clouds, melting the snowflakes falling on *PRB*'s white deck. Already that morning, Autissier had been outside stitching a tear in her mainsail. The canvas felt like ice; she was soaked and her hands were frozen. Back inside the cramped cabin, Autissier put on warm clothes. To dry out her spare boots, she fired up a small heater that her sister had given her.

Autissier thought about jibing the boat and adding a reef to her mainsail, but wanted to wait for the wind to swing to the west. Adjusting course at the wrong time would only be a waste of energy. She sat at her navigation table, where she often slept, and looked at charts. Outside, her autopilot steered *PRB* through steep swells.

Suddenly the wind shifted, and *PRB*'s sails whipped from one side of the boat to the other with a violent jerk. The bow plowed into a wave, and the boat turned on its side, slapping the water with a thunderous crack.

Autissier was thrown from her seat, but quickly recovered her footing. She lunged for the cabin hatch, clawing her way toward the boat's cockpit. With *PRB* on its side, she knew she had to get outside, ease the mainsail, and jibe. But by the time she opened the hatch, the boat had already rolled past ninety degrees, and the cockpit was almost upside down. She yanked the door shut and turned the handle to lock it. Then, *PRB*'s deck crashed onto the churning surface of the water.

Upside down now, Autissier crawled on *PRB*'s cabin ceiling. Peering out the windows, she could see her rig was still intact but pointing toward the ocean floor three miles down. She worked her way toward the controls for the hydraulic rams that moved her keel. She worked the keel back and forth, trying to flip the boat, but it was no good. She was running out of options; her mind raced.

to slingshot *FILA* toward Cape Horn. Besides, Soldini knew that if he tore up the boat, his race was over.

"We've been going pretty fast in the last forty-eight hours, though I haven't pushed the boat too hard," Soldini said in an e-mail to the ROC. "This is no time to be taking chances."

Autissier thought her strategy of staying to the south made more sense. And, for days, the wind remained a steady 22 mph, perfect sailing conditions. But on Sunday, February 14, she saw that the weather would turn.

"One more fast day behind the front, and we'll be hit by an-

What happened?

The conditions were not extreme, the wind not excessive. The boat shouldn't have capsized, she said to herself. Maybe the autopilot screwed up. It had given her problems before. *PRB* had another problem: It had a flat deck, which created suction when upside down. Newer generation Finots, like Thiercelin's and Hall's, have decks that are slightly bowed, making them easier to right. As a precaution, she had planned to install air bags on *PRB*'s stern. Once inflated, they would break the suction and make it easier to tip it back upright. In Auckland, however, Autissier and her crew decided the air bags took up too much deck space and didn't install them.

Autissier realized she wouldn't be able to right the boat. She crawled to her upside-down navigation station and tried to use her computer, which had been splashed with oil and water. The laptop still worked. She saw that Soldini and Thiercelin were her only hope; the rest of the fleet was more than 500 miles behind. A storm was approaching, so they would have to come quickly. As she looked at the chart, the computer shorted out. She picked up her satellite phone and punched in the number to her shore crew in France. The line crackled with static. She hung up and dialed her boyfriend's number. He couldn't make out what she was saying either. He yelled into the phone for her to shout some key words. He heard one: "Capsized!"

Autissier set off an emergency beacon, an electronic cry for help that would bounce off a satellite and into rescue offices and, ultimately, race headquarters in Charleston. Now all she could do was wait.

She watched through the windows of her cabin ceiling, now the floor, as the sea tore at the rig like a hungry shark. Then the mast broke off, and she feared it would puncture the deck. She put on her survival gear, an insulated outfit that would protect her from the thirty-eight-degree water. Then she crawled toward the life raft and the new escape hatch she had cut into *PRB*'s transom just before the race. She wanted to en-

sure she could make a quick escape if the boat began to sink.

It took a little while for the sadness to settle in. This was it for her beautiful boat. In the past three years, she had sailed 85,000 miles aboard *PRB*, 70,000 of those racing. Now, she looked around at a cabin splattered with oil and littered with gear. She knew she would abandon the boat. Still, she couldn't bear to see it messy. She began to clean up *PRB*'s cabin. Still a good boat, she said, mopping up with whatever she could find. Still a good boat.

And then, when she had done all she could do, she lay down on the cabin ceiling. It was cold inside the cabin, and only getting colder, but in the humid darkness she tried to sleep. She tried to dream about rescue.

Autissier installed the escape hatch on *PRB*'s transom just prior to this race.

PRB with life raft

Into The Wind

CHAPTER EIGHTEEN

Mark Schrader had only a half-hour to catch his over-booked connecting flight. He was jogging through Chicago's O'Hare International Airport, dragging bags of radios, computers and satellite phones when he heard the page.

"Mark Schrader - urgent message - please pick up a white courtesy telephone."

Schrader was on his way to Charleston for last-minute race business before flying to Punta del Este, Uruguay, to greet the Leg Three finishers. He didn't have much time to get to South America and set up for the first boats. Winding through the crowds of travelers stranded by the American Airlines pilots' strike, he finally found a phone. The message was short: Mark, call ROC immediately.

He felt a cold chill. Schrader knew one of his boats had to be in trouble. He called race coordinator Pete Dunning in Charleston.

"We've received an EPIRB alert from *PRB*. We've polled and messaged Isabelle but have received no reply," Dunning told him.

Suddenly, Schrader felt as if he had gone back in time. Four years before, he heard a similar message from Dunning about Harry Mitchell. This was the sort of emergency Schrader had feared since the race began. He hung up and ran to catch his plane. As the jet arced south toward the Carolinas, he tried to coordinate a rescue effort by air phone.

At first, race officials in Charleston weren't too worried about the EPIRB signal. In the past three months, three EPIRBs (emergency position-indicating radio beacons) had fired, each one a false alarm. They couldn't reach Autissier on her phone, but that wasn't so odd, either. Sometimes the phones didn't work; other skippers had been having troubles with theirs. It wasn't until they talked with technicians at ComSat Mobile Communications that they started to get anxious. A ComSat expert said Autissier's computer system had shut down without her properly logging off.

Then, a half-hour later, Autissier's French shore crew called and relayed the news about her boyfriend's report. Capsized.

Dunning's heart sank. Autissier couldn't be in a worse spot. Halfway between Cape Horn and New Zealand, Autissier was as close to the middle of nowhere as you can get. Weather reports forecasted 45-mph winds and forty-foot waves. She was 600 nautical miles south of the shipping lanes to Cape Horn. The ROC searched for vessels in the area and learned that one

Soldini on *FILA*

The message flashed on every computer screen in the fleet, though it really was meant only for two skippers: "We have received an EPIRB signal from Isabelle Autissier. *FILA* please contact race operations. *SOMEWHERE* please contact race operations."

J.P. Mouligne, one of Autissier's closest friends in the race, woke up to that message and thought he was still dreaming. Mouligne knew the situation was serious. Even if Autissier lost her mast, she wouldn't set off an EPIRB; she would simply set up a jury rig and start sailing. If Autissier asked for help, it was something worse. Mouligne wondered if his friend was still alive.

One hundred miles ahead of Autissier's last-known position, Marc Thiercelin had his own problems. In rough conditions, *SOMEWHERE* had busted its gooseneck, a metal fixture that holds the boom to the mast. Thiercelin noticed the gooseneck coming loose after *SOMEWHERE* suffered a violent knockdown, and knew it meant trouble. Without the boom, he would have limited use of his mainsail and that would cut down on the boat's maneuverability. And part of the safety factor of Finots is their ability to outrun bad weather and building-sized waves. Without its mainsail, *SOMEWHERE* would lose that safety margin.

Thiercelin had a solid lead over the rest of the fleet. On February 11, four days before Autissier capsized, he set a twenty-four-hour speed record for a monohull by sailing 393.3 nautical miles. It beat the old record set by Soldini just four months earlier. Three days later, Thiercelin bested his own record, sailing 396.5 nautical miles in a one-day period. "This is sailing right on the edge, with a very high level of stress," he said in a message to the ROC. "The ocean here is powerful. The waves are very high and steep, and everything lies under enormous clouds from Antarctica, loaded with hail and snow. The air is glacial, but the sunshine between the squalls magnificent."

Thiercelin was sailing through familiar waters. In the 1996-97 Vendee Globe, he had searched the same area for his friend

left Auckland on February 3 with a load of lamb meat bound for Portugal. But it was already around Cape Horn, more than 2,000 miles away. Race officials contacted the U.S. Navy. Maybe a submarine was in the area. They checked to see if NASA could get a satellite image of the Southern Ocean. But none of its satellites covered that part of the world. The whole Southern Pacific appeared to be deserted - except for the Around Alone skippers.

and fellow competitor, Gerry Roufs. Thiercelin had spent more than a day looking for Roufs, quitting only after race officials had twice ordered him to leave. In an e-mail to the ROC early on February 15, he noted the spot. "I may pass the way point on Tuesday morning, so I can expect to reach Cape Horn next Sunday," he said. "The way point is where Isa and I searched for Gerry Roufs two years ago. It gives me a weird feeling to be going back to the same place."

Thiercelin's uneasy feeling about that stretch of the Southern Ocean only grew stronger after he received the message about Autissier from the ROC. He called his shore crew in France. Embarrassed by his poor English, he knew it would be difficult to communicate over the satellite phone with the Americans in Charleston. He asked his shore crew to call the ROC and translate for him. They told him to keep working on the boat; Soldini was in a better position to rescue Autissier anyway. Thiercelin thought that was for the best. Based on the conditions, it appeared that Soldini could sail to Autissier's position more easily. Thiercelin would have to sail against the wind and the current, and he didn't know if his wounded gooseneck could take the punishment. He went back to work and continued on his course. It was a decision he would later regret.

Aboard *FILA*, Soldini was asleep in his bunk while the autopilot steered the boat. It was too cold to be out on deck. When he woke up and saw the ROC's message, he said to himself, "This is too much." He had lost his friend Andrea Romanelli overboard in an Atlantic storm the year before, and had just seen Luciano Nustrini crash and die in front of his boat. Now this. He knew it would be a battle to reach Autissier, but he didn't care. The bad luck had to stop. He had to try to do something. At nine-thirty that Monday morning, Soldini phoned the ROC.

"I'll go," he told Dunning.

Then he went on deck and turned *FILA* into the wind.

Soldini was 200 nautical miles northwest of Autissier's last known position when he diverted. Immediately, *FILA* was hit with 26-mph winds. The boat's bow crashed into the waves, each hit sounding like a gunshot. Soldini figured that he had twenty-four hours to go before he reached the location of Autissier's signal. He was now beating south as fast as *FILA*'s sixty feet of waterline would pull him. Ninety minutes after he diverted, Soldini went back inside and sent another message to race headquarters.

"I have thirty knots of wind, and I'm not letting up until I've found Isa."

Race officials believed Soldini was in a better position to rescue Autissier than Thiercelin. Schrader said it was the time, not the mileage, that determined who should go. Although Thiercelin was closer, Schrader thought it would take him longer to sail to *PRB*. Still, race officials felt Thiercelin should at least heave-to and wait for further instructions. Instead, *SOMEWHERE* was speeding in the opposite direction, toward Cape Horn. Now, Soldini was her only hope.

Soldini tried to sleep on the trip south, knowing he would need his energy later. But it was tough. He kept thinking about all the bad luck that had happened around him, hoping that this would be the turning point. He spent hours on the satellite phone with *PRB*'s shore crew, his shore crew, and Pierre Lasnier, his weather forecaster. Mouligne called to make sure Soldini had seen the message and told the Italian that he would divert *Cray Valley*, 450 miles astern of *FILA*. Most of the other skippers called in similar offers, but the next closest boat was at least two days away.

For six hours, *FILA* sailed into 45-mph headwinds, blasting through the endless mountain range of swells. *FILA* made more than seventeen knots, a great speed for a sailboat in any conditions. His course took him into the middle of a Southern Ocean storm whirling clockwise, sweeping across

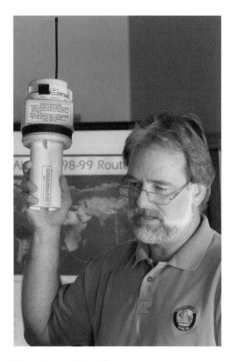

Race director Mark Schrader shows reporters an EPIRB (emergency position-indicating radio beacon) similar to the one on *PRB*.

FILA as the boat parted forty-foot waves. At one point, Soldini actually had to turn away from Autissier because the headwinds were too strong. But downwind he positioned himself to hit the search area just right. He'd been working out a search grid with his shore crew over the phone when he wasn't talking to *PRB*'s people in France. Visibility was about a half-mile, and even a three-mile search zone could take a week to cover. He didn't know how long Autissier would last.

Soldini knew that if he could get there fast, he had a chance to save her. *PRB* was emitting two signals, an EPIRB and a GPIRB (global position-indicating radio beacon), which can pinpoint a boat's location to within a few yards. The problem was those transmitters alone told Soldini and the ROC nothing except coordinates. Either one would keep signaling long after any survivors had been lost. But each boat also was equipped with an ARGOS signal, a long-lasting tracking device similar to the equipment scientists use to track whales. Autissier's ARGOS beacon was beeping. That was significant. To activate the ARGOS, you have to unscrew a medicine bottle-sized cap, reach inside and flip a switch. It took a person to do that. She had to be alive. That only comforted race officials so much, though. The water temperature was near freezing in the Southern Ocean summer, the wind blowing so hard it sheared whitecaps off the swells. Conditions were getting worse, and one of Autissier's tracking beacons had cut off. Race officials hoped it was just her way to conserve batteries.

At midnight in the Southern Ocean, Soldini was twenty-five miles from the last position anyone had for *PRB*. He switched on *FILA*'s radar, which had a range of thirty-six miles. If Autissier was out there, Soldini thought he could find her.

"I have hope for the moment," Soldini said in a message to race headquarters at 1:43 a.m on February 16, "but I don't see anything now."

Soldini had to sail smart. Currents were pushing *PRB* east. If he miscalculated, he would have to turn *FILA* around and backtrack. He had to sail downwind of Autissier and let the current take him in.

In February, the Southern Ocean sunrise comes at about 4:00 a.m. As Soldini reached Autissier's last-known position, it was almost dawn. He didn't see anything. He drew up plans to search each square of his grid. He worried that he would miss her in the giant swells. She could be behind any one of countless waves.

As daylight squeezed through the clouds, Soldini was ready to sail off and begin his search. When he started to turn the boat, he caught something out of the corner of his eye. He turned around and peered into the gray waves.

There it was, the black bottom of *PRB*'s hull, its keel standing in the air like a stubby mast. Capsized, but in one piece. He had found it.

"Isabelle!"

Soldini shouted for her as loud as he could, but it was no good. If she was inside her boat, she couldn't hear anything over the water sloshing around the hull, especially Soldini's tenor voice a hundred yards away. He would have to move in closer.

It was a tricky piece of sailing. Soldini could not risk bumping *PRB*'s hull with *FILA*. He sailed back and forth, yelling Autissier's name.

Once. Twice. Nothing.

Soldini knew he needed something louder. He looked around *FILA*'s cramped quarters. Then he spied his toolbox. And in it, his hammer.

Soldini would later shrug off what he did next. "I threw the hammer very strong, and that's it," he explained.

It wasn't quite that simple. He had one shot to hit a black hull floating in dark water on a gray, foggy Southern Ocean morning. He hurled the hammer across the water. It connected loudly.

Bonk!

Autissier had been asleep, not expecting anyone to reach her position so soon. She was cold, still lying on the cabin's ceiling, still in the dark. She had stirred moments before, think-ing she heard something. But inside *PRB*, the noise was deaf-ening with the waves pelting the hull.

Then she heard the hammer hit, which she later described as "this perfect noise."

Autissier scrambled to the hatch in *PRB's* transom. She opened it and looked outside. *FILA* shone on the water like a white horse. On its deck, the short, bearded Soldini jumped up and down, waving and smiling.

As Autissier scrambled out of *PRB's* escape hatch, the seas calmed a little - just enough for Soldini to throw her a rope. She caught it and climbed into the life raft she had tied to the boat's stern. She stepped off *PRB* for the last time and let Soldini pull her to *FILA*.

At the ROC, they hadn't heard anything for ten minutes. They didn't know what Soldini would find when he got to *PRB*, whether Autissier needed medical attention, or if he could even get her off the boat. It was 6:00 a.m. in the South-ern Ocean, Soldini had been in position about two hours. What, they wondered, was going on? Then, the ROC received a simple message from Soldini.

"hallo this is fila, isabel is in board wit mi everythinc is ok, wi are going to tek isi end go bak in the race ciao gio"

On board *FILA*, Soldini prepared the cold but unhurt Autissier a glass of wine and some cheese. Soldini told her to take it easy, and gave her some FILA foul-weather gear. Then he steered *FILA* back on a course east, toward Cape Horn. Within a couple of hours, they were joking about being short on wine and cheese.

When Soldini set off after the rescue, he was nearly 400 miles behind Thiercelin, almost certainly out of contention for the leg and probably the race. The best he could do was sec-ond place. It was a fate that bothered his fans more than Soldi-ni. A day after the rescue, Dan McConnell told Soldini in a

Autissier and Soldini shortly after the rescue.

phone conversation that people were upset that misfortune had cost Soldini a race that many people expected him to win.

But the Italian skipper didn't care.

"I've already won," Soldini told McConnell. "I saved Isabelle."

A Southern Ocean storm from the cockpit of *Balance Bar*

Stormy Weather

T he Around Alone skippers hurtled east through the Southern Pacific, eager to get the 4,500 miles between New Zealand and South America behind them. As they dipped south, they scanned the horizon for growlers, small icebergs that were a threat even in February, the height of summer in the Southern Hemisphere. And they had to stay alert for the constant shifts in the area's treacherous weather. Every day, the waves grew larger and the winds stronger, the two conspiring to knock the boats around like bathtub toys. It was the roughest weather some of the skippers had ever seen.

On February 13, Viktor Yazykov's *Wind of Change* was tearing through heavy seas at twelve knots, so fast that the bow jutted out of the water as the boat skimmed across the waves. *Wind of Change* was designed like a smaller version of the sixty-foot Finots, and it took to the Southern Ocean conditions well. But a thousand miles into Leg Three, the Russian was shaken when a floating log hit the bottom of the boat. It missed his keel and rudder by inches.

"Still no sign of any damage," Yazykov said in an e-mail to the ROC. "Would like to dive and check it in calm."

Yazykov would never get the chance, though. The weather never let up, and the ocean exploited every weakness in his tiny yacht. A wind-direction indicator that he had installed in Auckland was torn from the masthead in a knockdown. A solar panel, which helped generate electricity for his communications systems, washed overboard. Once, his boom slammed into the deck and he felt lucky to find no damage.

At times, Yazykov's boat topped twenty-five knots, an amazing speed for a forty-foot sailboat. Surfing along two days later, *Wind of Change* crashed onto its side, and the Russian had to slowly haul in his mainsail to right the boat. It was a ritual he would repeat several times a day until, finally, Yazykov gave up on the idea of diving to check his hull.

"I have been scared to death," he said in an e-mail. "Thought the boat was going to completely capsize."

After Autissier's fate, capsizing was a common fear throughout the fleet. Skippers kept their sails furled for days at a time. The wind on the bare mast and the current were enough to push the boats along as fast as many skippers felt comfortable sailing. Knockdowns became so common the skippers stopped counting them. And it only got worse. The fleet's weather forecaster on February 18 told the sailors to hold on tight. A massive low-pressure system with sustained winds of 55 mph and gusts in the sixties was about to hit them head-on.

The strongest winds were on the outer edges of the storm, which stretched hundreds of miles across. It was a gigantic system, noteworthy even by Southern Ocean standards. Worse, it was about to merge with another storm coming from the opposite direction. The bulk of the fleet would be stuck between the two systems when they collided.

Shortly after that ominous forecast arrived aboard *Magellan Alpha*, Mike Garside got a call from the Chilean Coast Guard, asking him to divert to a vessel in distress. Garside jibed, and *Magellan* took off on its new heading. As soon as he looked at the coordinates, however, Garside realized he was being diverted to Isabelle Autissier's abandoned, capsized *PRB*. He called the ROC for help. He did not want to turn from his intercept course until the people in Chile knew they had a false alarm. In the hour it took to clear up the situation, Garside was distracted. *Magellan Alpha* wasn't balanced well when the storm descended on him. When it hit, *Magellan*, steered by autopilot, did a nosedive into a wave.

Garside landed in the bunk on his back, laptop computer in his hands. Regaining his footing, he looked out the window to see his mast, mainsail and genoa go in the water. The wind pinned *Magellan* on its side for half an hour and Garside had no idea when, or if, it would right itself. Remembering Autissier's fate, he waited for the moment he would hear the sharp crack and see his rigging sink into the frigid depths. But, after a while, just past ninety degrees, *Magellan Alpha* popped back up.

A couple of days later, Garside received an e-mail from Brad Van Liew. The two skippers and class rivals had become good friends and talked daily, either by e-mail or on the single sideband radios all the boats carried. They were complete opposites. Garside mostly kept to himself, and when he talked, his voice was a snarl dripping with British wit. Van Liew was gregarious, outgoing and younger than Garside's daughter. But

they shared one thing in common: They were both sick of the Southern Ocean.

When the storm forecast came over Van Liew's computer, he sent an e-mail to Ken Campbell at Commander's Weather: Just how bad is this storm? The message that came back chilled him like an Antarctic breeze.

"Brad, I would not want to be you right now," Campbell replied. "Looks to me like you could be in for a real rough ride."

Van Liew took the warning seriously. He battened down everything on *Balance Bar*, stored everything that was loose. He was too far behind the storm to run, too far ahead to turn north. Over the next few days, as the Southern Ocean knocked Van Liew and *Balance Bar* around like a volleyball, he kept a storm diary:

18 February: I'm screwed. ... I am in no-man's land, bobbing around in a tiny boat and a giant storm is bearing down on me. No one in the world can help me except maybe my fellow competitors.

19 February: It can only be a short time now before I get the first punch in the chops. Winds picking up ... 40 knots, 45, 50 knots sustained with some stronger gusts. Conditions outside are ugly, snow and sleet. Thank God for my two trusty autopilots.

21 February: I went on deck to check everything and cinch everything down even tighter. I have used every sail tie to secure the main, lowered the boom and cinched it down, too. I am sailing under bare poles.

22 February: Long night. Can't sleep with all the banging and bucking. ... Gusts have now moved into the 100-knot range. And the winds have clocked around almost 180 degrees. The seas have become horrific. The 40-foot waves created by the earlier northwest winds are still coming at me from that direction while new waves created by the southeast winds are hitting me from the opposite directions. It's ugly. Everything is white. Snow, hail and sea-foam all blowing horizontally across my field of vision. I am surrounded by the most fearsome seas. I am not feeling too good about the boat's ability to survive such abuse. It feels like I am seeing something very few people survive to see.

26 February: I am really getting my ass kicked now ... recalibrated the autopilot, and we are now sailing at 7 knots under bare poles. Even without an inch of sail up, I am overpowered and there's not a damn thing I can do about it. Does anyone know how to reef a mast? Winds are 70 knots sustained, with gusts most likely of 100 knots or more. The gusts are indescribable. I have never felt anything like it in all my years of sailing. When one hits, *Balance Bar* just shudders. The seas have reached a dangerous state. Waves are over 40 feet heading in opposite directions. When two of these giants collide, they create an enormous mountain of water that towers ABOVE my 80-foot mast. They break after they merge and there is no apparent rhyme or reason to which way they break. The boat is bucking and heaving constantly. I am eliminating many normal tasks, even body functions. I'm thirsty, but I'm limiting my body fluids.

27 February: We are in the death zone. Things are out of control. I can do no more. I've been spending a lot of time in my foul-weather bunk. It's about eight feet long and 24 inches square. It's enclosed on the right by the starboard hull and on the left by the engine compartment bulkhead. The ceiling is in the cockpit sole. When the boat gets knocked over or rolls, I can't go anywhere. I just bounce around in this box like a bean in a baby rattle. ... It's too rough to even think about preparing a meal. I'd have to duct tape the food down to the pot to cook it. I am living on Balance Bars.

What is happening now is truly frightening. When *Balance Bar* happens to be where two waves collide, the boat is lifted to the very top of the combined wave. It's like riding a fast elevator up to the 10th floor of an office building. I just feel the boat going up. Then it sits there suspended while the wave makes up its mind which way it's going to break. Suddenly *Balance Bar* flops down on her side and

surfs sideways down the face of the wave. It's now happening at least twice an hour.

28 February: I really flipped out a little while ago. The boat got hit again, and I just started punching the bulkhead in a fury, yelling, "Stop it ... just knock it the hell off ... no more, no more!"

I was sitting here (at the nav station) just watching the instruments when I felt the boat rise on another wave. I wedged my feet under the nav station, pressed one hand on the ceiling, and grabbed the windward side of the nav desk with the other and braced myself. The boat reached the top and hung there. Then "bang" she went over on her side. Tons of white water engulfed *Balance Bar*, throwing her so far and so fast that GPS satellites hundreds of miles overhead registered the event. ... In just eight seconds the GPS showed the boat sailing SIDEWAYS AT 15 KNOTS! The boat wasn't simply surfing sideways down these waves but was actually getting trapped on the tunnel of rushing water that crashed down the side of the wave. Frightening. Losing the mast had become a likely possibility.

In the middle of the storm

When *Balance Bar* was thrown past ninety degrees in one knockdown, Van Liew found himself staring out his cabin windows into the deep blue depths of the Southern Ocean. He could take no more. He sent Garside an e-mail.

"I am really getting it. I don't know how much more of this the boat or I can take. We are really losing it down here."

Garside responded quickly. His message was short and to the point:

"Brad: You are NOT alone. I am just 120 miles from you. I can reach you in 24 hours if it becomes necessary. Hang in there. The storm will pass."

The impact of the storm was beginning to take a toll on Van

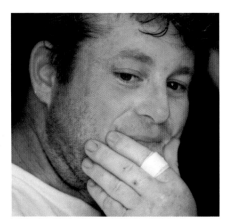

Van Liew

Liew. He watched supposedly unbreakable dishes fly across the cabin and hit the hull's inner wall so hard that they shattered. Books, digital cameras and knick-knacks littered the floor.

28 February: My personal condition is deteriorating alarmingly. I haven't eaten anything for so long now I can't remember. I am covered in cuts and bruises. I haven't washed or brushed my teeth in two days. Both the boat and I are undergoing a slow but steady degradation. We are both beaten down, beaten down, beaten down. ... The bully outside is still wailing on us.

28 February: I am in pitch darkness, the boat sliding off the top of five-story high waves, crawling around on deck trying to figure out what's making that noise. The spinnaker pole had popped loose on deck. I lash it back down. I climb back into my bunk. I settle in. Then there's this godawful rapping noise right over my head. The wind is blowing in excess of 70 knots. I trudge back on deck. Turns out it was the jack line that runs from the bow to the stern. I snap my safety harness, too. The wind is blowing so hard that it's snapping against the deck sounding like a rifle shot each time it hits. I freak out. I mean, I really lose it! Instead of just securing the line I pull out my knife and cut the damn thing in rage. Dumb, but it felt like somehow I had at least taken a swing at the beast.

28 February: After almost 60 hours of hell the winds are dropping. I know I should be putting up sail now, I am apprehensive. I feel a kind of post-traumatic syndrome. I don't know if "scared" is the right word. I wait. But for what? This is nuts. I'm in a damn race. I have to get the sails up ... but still I sit here and find good excuses.

Van Liew thought about Harry Mitchell and Gerry Roufs, and tried to motivate himself to keep racing. The boat had suffered no major damage. Van Liew cleaned up the cabin and tried to prepare himself mentally to get back in the race. He sent another message to Garside.

"Thanks for the encouragement the last three days. I am back on my feet so you better put your turbo-charger on because I'm coming after you."

Hundreds of miles ahead, *FILA* was out of the worst weather. But Soldini and Autissier were dealing with their own storm. Just after she was rescued from her capsized *PRB*, Autissier had made the remark "We're going cruising together." In France, where singlehanded sailing is taken more seriously than in most places, a few professional skippers and news reports were critical of Autissier's comment, and her sailing skills. To some, it sounded as if Autissier meant to help Soldini.

Aboard *SOMEWHERE*, 500 miles east of *FILA*, Marc Thiercelin received a call from a reporter asking him about the situation. At the time, Thiercelin was tired, stressed out and busy planning a rendezvous with his shore crew around Cape Horn to make better repairs to his gooseneck and boom. *SOMEWHERE* also had pitched over after a crash-jibe so violent that it broke his laptop computer. He was not in the best mood to answer questions.

Thiercelin said he was sorry that Autissier had capsized, but he felt that she was messing up Soldini's race by remaining onboard *FILA*. He had offered, through race officials, to have his shore crew pick up Autissier near Cape Horn, where they would be working on *SOMEWHERE*. Ultimately, Thiercelin said, Autissier capsized because she "screwed up."

"She isn't realistic," he told the publication *Le Figaro*. "If only she didn't haul on her boat like a mule."

Thiercelin was irritated that he could lose his lead in the race by a liberal time compensation that a fawning race committee might give Soldini for his heroics. "The settling up will be done after we arrive. That just isn't done. I sweated bullets, and I don't feel like having my victory gambled away." Thiercelin also said that Mark Schrader should have told Autissier to keep her mouth shut. But perhaps, he said, she wasn't thinking. She was tired and dazed. It was the same thing Autissier would later say about Thiercelin's comments.

The Around Alone rules are simple: If a skipper rescues someone, the passenger does not help sail the boat. Cooking, cleaning and companionship are fine. Just no hauling on halyards. Race veterans, Autissier and Soldini knew the rules well. They helped draft them. Race officials wanted the entire issue dropped. It was horrible publicity. Race spokesman Dan McConnell said there was no controversy. All his skippers are people of honor, he argued.

Autissier had no plans to get off *FILA* at Cape Horn. She felt it was too dangerous. Navigating close to the Horn would only complicate Soldini's race and slow him down. And, Soldini would get no credit for all the time it would take letting her off the boat.

But aboard *FILA*, Soldini and Autissier said they didn't even really consider themselves racing anymore. They had mixed feelings about the controversy, and even the race. The whole incident had changed their priorities. All they wanted to do was sail safely to Punta del Este. Stuck inside the cramped cabin of *FILA*, Autissier and Soldini talked about old times the way friends do, sipped tea and swapped stories. They discussed their childhood dreams. They talked about life, the sea and sailing. One day, Soldini talked about the loss of his friend, Andrea Romanelli, and how bad he felt about it. Autissier tried to console him. When Soldini was sleeping or working on the boat, Autissier sent e-mails to many of the skippers to offer them advice and support.

"She would say, 'Hey, I hope everything's good. I see a storm's coming, are you going to be OK?' or 'Hey, this is what you need to do when you get here.' She's a friend," Van Liew said later.

In all, Soldini felt it was the best two weeks of sailing he'd ever had. He was happy to have rescued Autissier. But he was as infuriated by press accounts calling him a hero as he was by those accusing him of cheating. If a freighter had rescued her,

would they have called the captain of that ship a hero? Soldini thought not. He felt he was only doing his job as a seaman.

The two sailors laughed at the picture of themselves being painted by the international press: the two of them working from *FILA*'s cockpit, cranking on winches, changing sails, trying desperately to catch Thiercelin. The reality was very different. The boat was on autopilot, and they rarely ventured outside the cabin.

Soldini and Autissier en route to Cape Horn

But Soldini's explosive temper grew as the controversy continued to unfold. Soldini loved the Around Alone race and hated to see negative stories as a result of something he had done. He called race director Mark Schrader in Punta del Este.

"Listen, if there is a serious problem, I will be out of the race," Soldini told Schrader. "It's not a problem for me. I'll just do the fourth leg and I'll beat him in the fourth leg and that's it."

No way, Schrader replied. Schrader could tell Soldini had let things get to him. He was tired, sailing through dangerous waters, and he was being attacked for something that he had been praised for the day before. Schrader told Soldini that the controversy was silly. Ignore it.

"He was afraid it was affecting the rest of the race," Schrader said later.

Soldini kept up his new lifestyle after that, cooking pasta for himself and Autissier as *FILA* shaved off the miles to Cape Horn. And slowly, as Soldini closed on the southern tip of South America, he started gaining on Thiercelin.

INTO THE WIND

Cape Horn

Steered by autopilot, *Cray Valley* sailed into Drake Passage on a Friday afternoon while J.P. Mouligne took a nap in his bunk. It was February 26, a day Mouligne had anticipated for twenty years.

On the chart table, Mouligne's VHF radio crackled to life as it picked up a signal. As Mouligne shook off the sleep, he recognized the language was Spanish and remembered that the VHF has a range of only about fifteen miles. He had to be close to land. Mouligne jumped up, looked out the window on the starboard side of the cabin and saw, ten miles away, the little island of Diego Ramirez. It still amazed him to sail across thousands of miles of water and then find land on the horizon, just where the chart said it would be.

As Mouligne peered out at Diego Ramirez, barren save for a lighthouse, he realized he had made it. He knew that off the port bow, spiking out of the sea, was Cape Horn. But he didn't look, he wanted to wait until he was closer. Since he was a child, Mouligne had dreamed of seeing the Horn. He wanted his first image of it to be impressive; he knew he would savor that sight forever. So, careful not to glance out the other side of the boat, he sat back down.

Inside *Cray Valley*'s cabin, Mouligne fidgeted like a boy waiting for Christmas morning. He held out for almost thirty minutes. Wrestling into his foul-weather gear, Mouligne finally climbed out of the cabin and onto the deck. It was four-thirty in the afternoon and as usual, the weather was rough. *Cray Valley* sailed into headwinds. It was cold, and the sea was choppy. Not a very friendly place, Mouligne thought. But, through the mist and the spray, he saw it.

"It was just a huge triangle rising out of the fog," he said later. "It was about fifteen miles away. I was too far. I wish I could have come right to it. But it was too rough. Still, you see it perfectly. It's an amazing place."

Towering out of the mist, Cape Horn looms over the border of the Pacific and the Atlantic like a giant gravestone. A huge, black pyramid, the 600-foot barren face of the Horn is the southern tip of South America. At 56 degrees latitude, Cape Horn marks the north side of Drake Passage, a narrow stretch of water between Chile and Antarctica. Here the seas spin around the bottom of the planet and funnel into a 500-mile, shallow channel that builds and stacks huge, cresting waves. Rounding the Horn is a rite of passage that sailors have celebrated for centuries with a gold hoop earring. They do not earn the right to wear the earring easily.

Gale-force winds churn the sea viciously around the Horn, and much of the time the landmark is shrouded in fog. Often skippers sail by without ever seeing it, but they can sense its presence. Many sailors who dreamed their entire lives of seeing the Horn have had to steer just out of sight once they were close. The danger of being smashed against rocks or running aground around the Horn is too great.

Before the Panama Canal opened in 1914, rounding the Horn was the shortest way to get from Europe to California. When the gold rush hit in the 1840s, hundreds of triple-masted sailing ships rounded the Horn every year, and many more failed trying. In one particularly bad year, 130 ships set sail from Europe to the west coast of the United States, and only fifty-two made it.

Sir Arthur H. Rostron, the captain of the *Carpathia*, the luxury liner that rescued *Titanic*'s survivors, began his career as a hand on the barkentines that routinely traveled the route. In his autobiography, *Home From The Sea*, Rostron said he was haunted by something he saw near the Horn while battling a gale aboard the clipper ship *Cedric the Saxon*.

"As the boat pitched like a cork and all hands aloft were struggling to furl sail, out of the murky smother about us we saw flares burning," Rostron wrote. "We were passing another ship in dire distress, worse, far worse, than we were. I often wonder what happened to her; we never knew who she was or what her fate. It looked as though she writhed in her death throes, there within a cable's length of us. And we could do nothing. ... Sometimes when I have glanced at that terribly long list of missing ships I wonder whether her name is upon it somewhere."

The wooden ships that litter the floor of the ocean near the Horn are never far from the minds of skippers who sail through Drake Passage. In some ways, Cape Horn is more isolated now, thanks to air cargo and the Panama Canal. That makes it more dangerous because fewer people are around to rescue a skipper in trouble.

The Around Alone skippers knew that all too well, and approached the Horn cautiously. But the thrill of sailing close to Cape Horn held the same appeal to them as orbiting the moon has to an astronaut. They wanted to see it, to be close to it.

Not all the skippers felt the rush that overcame Mouligne, but they all noted their passing. Viktor Yazykov said that in Cold War-era Russia, when most people were forbidden to leave the country, Cape Horn was like a star. You could see it out there, but you could not touch it. Brad Van Liew had not thought much about seeing the Horn until he got there after surviving a storm he had not expected to get through. To British skipper and former soldier Mike Garside, a man not easily impressed, "It was just another bloody rock in the sea." For most, however, it meant a little more. Even though the water around Cape Horn was dangerous, it was a welcome sight to the sailors. It signaled the end of their Southern Ocean voyage. A turn to the north after the Horn steered the fleet into the South Atlantic Ocean, which is relatively calm off the coast of Argentina.

Marc Thiercelin was the first in the fleet to see the Horn. It was his second rounding since January 1997, when he sailed by during the last Vendee Globe. This time he was planning a pit stop with his shore crew at Tierra del Fuego just north of the Horn. He made little effort to do any sightseeing. He shaved close to Cape Horn to save on miles with *SOMEWHERE* doing nine knots in choppy seas.

"So here I am, for the second time ... rounding this pebble, this rock at the end of the world known as Cape Horn," Thiercelin said in an e-mail to the ROC. "The sky is overcast and the sea gray and confused, but the gale I was sailing into yesterday has passed. While I was crawling along pounding into the waves, *FILA* was approaching from above with the depression, and doing sixteen or eighteen knots on a reach. Hello! I have lost a large part of my lead as a result."

Soldini was earning his second gold hoop as well. When *FILA* rounded the Horn just a day behind *SOMEWHERE*, Soldini realized it was the exact day he'd first rounded the Horn four years earlier, February 23. That was during the 1994-95 race, when he finished second in Class Two behind David Adams. Now, he was stuck behind Thiercelin for the Class One lead. But Soldini liked his chances this time. In the last week, *FILA* had sailed through better weather and made up 300 miles on *SOMEWHERE*. Now Soldini trailed by only 100 miles. He thought about the race as the day ended, the setting sun painting the black rock with brilliant colors.

Autissier was on deck with Soldini. Looking out at the Horn four miles away, she was saddened when she began to think about her lost boat, *PRB*. She had never expected her fifth rounding of Cape Horn to be aboard *FILA*. For a week, Autissier and Soldini had put the race out of their minds, talking and reminiscing in the boat's cabin. Now, as they rounded the Horn, the race felt as real as the rock jutting out of the sea in front of them. The rest of the race, she knew, would be about tactics up the coast of South America, and Soldini was already thinking about his strategy. Autissier was more alone now, just a passenger, and the Horn was just another reminder that she was out of the race. She spoke to it as *FILA* sailed past.

"I'll be back old man," she said.

Neal Petersen had waited nearly as long as Mouligne to see the Horn, and the final hours of his journey were the toughest. As he approached the landmark on the night of March 11, *www.no-barriers.com* was tossed around in thirty-foot seas. Steady 70-mph winds pounded the little red boat, and Petersen clocked one gust at 84 mph.

Scared of being rolled, Petersen pushed the boat downwind into Drake Passage. He surfed off waves at fifteen knots - so fast that he sometimes hit others from behind. Petersen kept

himself attached to the boat with a two-foot tether, a short leash. He couldn't see the waves chasing him, but he could hear them. Each time, he would take a deep breath, pray his tether wouldn't break and hang on. Soon he was drenched in ice-cold, chest-deep water that crashed into the boat's cockpit. But the little homemade boat held together.

"How we did not roll over, I don't know," he would later say.

The gale ripped his mainsail and knocked the boat back and forth as if it were a punching bag. During the worst part of the storm, Petersen struggled to furl all his sails, but the current and the wind on the boat's bare rigging were enough to move it at a ten-knot clip. As he worked, the spray stung his eyes, and he breathed in water as if he were diving into the sea.

The boat was trashed. Twelve inches of water flooded the cabin. It was pitch black and Petersen had to use a flashlight to see anything. His fingers were so cold he couldn't hold the tiller. Exhausted, soaked and cold, Petersen dove into the cabin. While he was below warming up, the wind and the waves battered the boat. Petersen stopped counting the knockdowns at twelve. To cushion the blows, he hugged pillows and covered himself with a wet sleeping bag. He thought about his girlfriend, Gwen Wilkinson.

"Dear Gwen, I am alive," he wrote in an e-mail to her after the storm. "Never before have I had to fight for my life like last night. I will try to get the boat cleaned up, but first I need some sleep and warmth. I have been shivering all night, and have hypothermia. I now wish the heater was working as I could do with its warmth. Oh well, I am alive, I survived. I thought of you throughout the night and wondered what daylight would bring me."

On March 13, it was typically gray and foggy as Petersen sailed within two miles of the Horn. Twenty-one years earlier, when he was just ten, Petersen began reading the stories of Joshua Slocum's trip around the world. Now, Petersen had achieved a personal dream. He had joined that elite fraternity

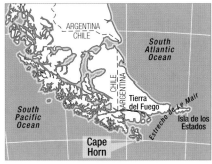

Petersen at The Horn

of singlehanded sailors to round the Horn. His hair in tangles from the rough trip across the Southern Pacific, Petersen set up a camera to record the moment and snapped a frame of him with the Horn just over his shoulder.

For Petersen, sailing around Cape Horn was just more proof of the message he preached to schoolchildren. It was the theme of the e-mail he sent to the ROC with the Horn off his port bow.

"If I could come from the background where I come from, with the few tools I had, and achieve my goal, then the billions of youth out in this world too can make their dreams a reality," he said.

As Petersen wrote, the wind dropped to an easy five knots. He looked outside and smiled to himself. He felt like it was Cape Horn's way of wishing him a good passage.

Minoru Saito left Auckland with a clear purpose. Saito wanted to join the ranks of the few skippers who had completed three solo circumnavigations and knew that making it through the Southern Pacific would be his biggest obstacle. But he had another mission as well.

The 65-year-old Japanese skipper was haunted by the death of Harry Mitchell. Mitchell had disappeared during the last race before he tried to round Cape Horn. Saito had been near Mitchell, but with his generator out, he had no power for his radio. Mitchell might have called for help, Saito thought, and he might have saved him if he'd had his radio on.

Saito planned to sail to Mitchell's last-known position and throw a gold hoop earring overboard for the lost sailor. With the weather battering him and the rear of the fleet taking a more northerly course, Saito steered *Shuten-dohji II* south for his rendezvous. On March 3, Saito neared the spot when a storm with winds reaching 100 mph pummeled his yacht. "Bloody weather," he cursed in broken English in an e-mail to the ROC.

"*Shuten-dohji II* has many times knockdown, too much messy in a cabin," he said. "Still not sails, but boat speeds about seven or eight knots."

The wind ripped the sails on Saito's old yacht and, for five minutes, a 107-mph gust plastered it against the water. He looked at the readout on a wind instrument ... 94 mph, 95, 97, 98 .... "Crazy," he said.

Twice Saito tried to turn his boat into the wind, determined to reach the exact spot where his friend had disappeared. Both times he was stopped.

"I cannot get to the area unfortunately," Saito said in an e-mail to the ROC. "Now back to northeast."

His sails in tatters, Saito changed course and headed for Cape Horn.

On March 12, Saito rounded the Horn for the third time. The weather cooperated on this day. With light winds, Saito sailed within a half-mile of Cape Horn, closer than he had ever been. The seas were only three feet and the sun briefly shone through the clouds. There, Saito made his peace with Mitchell, toasting him with sake and tossing a gold earring into the sea. He took the other one of the pair and put it in the cabin, saving it for Mitchell's widow, Diana. He would give it to her when he got back to Charleston.

Before he sailed on, though, Saito performed one more ceremony. A decade earlier, Saito had lost his girlfriend in a sailboat accident off Hawaii. She had always wanted to see the Horn, and he promised her he would one day make it so. Thinking about that unfulfilled promise, Saito toasted his lost love with more sake, looked at the Horn once more, and steered for the South Atlantic.

SOMEWHERE
off South America

CHAPTER TWENTY ONE

Marc Thiercelin stood on the deck of *SOMEWHERE*, staring out over Aguirre Bay as his lead melted away. Hours before, his shore crew had arrived in this remote area of Tierra del Fuego, Argentina, aboard a chartered yacht, and now they scrambled to fix the boat's gooseneck. The repairs were taking longer than Thiercelin had estimated, and that made him uneasy. Every minute he was stopped, Giovanni Soldini was catching up. But he knew that without the repairs, he could not win the leg.

In the Southern Ocean, Thiercelin had sailed fast even with his broken gooseneck. He lashed lines to the boom to control its movement, and the set-up had worked fine with a reefed mainsail. But now he needed the ability to move his boom and completely unfurl his mainsail to keep moving fast in light winds. A few hours earlier, when he had rounded Cape Horn, he sent a message about his situation to the ROC.

"I have to remain in the lead, where I have been since Auckland, but also stop so as to be able to continue," he said. "Life is an eternal contradiction."

As his fifth hour at anchor passed, Thiercelin grew anxious. He had expected to be stopped for only four hours. On his computer plots, he could see Soldini tearing along at seventeen knots, eating away at a lead that days before had been

greater than 400 miles. *FILA* was now just 288 miles away.

Thiercelin sailed out of Aguirre Bay after six hours. As soon as he was back in open water, he was hit by strong northerly winds that kept him from pushing *SOMEWHERE* through the dangerous, rocky Straits of Le Maire. He instead had to sail east, around Isla de los Estados, which took him more than a hundred miles out of his way. And when he got to the windward side of the island, *SOMEWHERE* coasted into a windless hole south of the Falkland Islands. Before Thiercelin could catch a good breeze, Soldini closed to within ninety miles by cutting through the straits.

The next day Thiercelin and Soldini finally got their chance to race. *FILA* and *SOMEWHERE* tacked up the coast of Argentina, Thiercelin mirroring Soldini's every move. Herb McCormick, the race's senior media correspondent, said the French skipper was employing the most basic race tactic: Stay between your opponent and the finish line. One-thousand miles from Punta del Este, Soldini had closed to within seventy-eight miles. Every minute counted.

Overnight, Thiercelin managed to pull away from Soldini again, and by the next morning he had extended his lead to 200 miles.

Thiercelin talked with French reporters on his satellite phone

Thiercelin

as *SOMEWHERE*'s autopilot steered the yacht through rough seas in 30-mph winds. It was early morning off the coast of Argentina. Punta was now just 800 miles away and it looked as if he would have a solid, eighteen-hour overall lead going into the last leg, from Uruguay back to Charleston. He was poised to win his first around-the-world singlehanded race.

And then, with a crack, it all fell apart.

SOMEWHERE's mast broke. The carbon fiber spar jumped off the ball that swiveled it, broke in two and speared the boat's cabin. One piece crashed through the ceiling and navigation station where Thiercelin sat. He jumped out of the way just in time.

"I was lucky my head was not cut off in the incident," he would say later.

Water poured into *SOMEWHERE*'s cabin through two holes: the one where the mast had been, and the one it made when it fell. Thiercelin's computer shorted out and his navigation station flooded. He went on deck and began to cut the mast away.

Race operations heard about *SOMEWHERE*'s dismasting from Thiercelin's shore crew after the skipper sent a simple message through his team in Paris. The shore crew assured officials at the ROC that Thiercelin didn't think the boat was in danger.

Race operations sent a message about Thiercelin's predicament to the fleet. Most were too far away to help. Only *FILA*, with one rescued skipper already onboard, was close enough to help. Soldini responded instantly.

"Received the news of the dismasting, tell us if you need anything," Soldini wrote in a message to Pete Dunning, the race coordinator.

Thiercelin tried to downplay the danger, but Mark Schrader would take no chances. With *SOMEWHERE* likely to lose its communications equipment, he decided the best thing to do was to divert Soldini, who was already on an intercept course. The race officials called Soldini back and, once again, *FILA* was off to the rescue.

The rescue mission lasted only an hour, though. Through his shore crew, Thiercelin told race headquarters that he didn't need any help. He would set up a jury rig and sail to the Falkland Islands. There he would rendezvous with his shore crew and step a new mast. He would not withdraw from the race. Soldini was released from his diversion, and *FILA* steered back into the light air off Argentina.

Thiercelin wrestled with his rigging for twenty hours, experimenting with different jury rigs, trying to find one that would push *SOMEWHERE* through the water. He had decided to set course for Port Stanley on the east side of the windward Falkland Island, about 200 miles away. He could work on the boat there but wouldn't be able to make permanent repairs. *SOMEWHERE* had a ninety-foot mast, and no planes flew into the Falklands that could stow a mast that long. He would have to settle for a smaller one, and replace it in Uruguay. He called his shore crew and told them to find the best mast they could and meet him there in a few days.

And then Thiercelin, exhausted, slept for four hours before

he began his slow sail toward the Falkland Islands.

With the Southern Ocean behind them, the skippers thought the rest of the Around Alone would be an easy cruise up the coast of the Americas. They were wrong. A few days after *SOMEWHERE* dismasted, Mike Garside stood on the deck of *Magellan Alpha* waiting for his drifting boat to be impaled on the rocks only a few hundred yards away. Garside had cut through the Straits of Le Maire, a twenty-mile channel between the Isla de los Estados and Tierra del Fuego, to save himself nearly 100 miles. But once Garside turned into the passage the wind died, and the currents began to push him east. Through the night, Garside scanned the horizon, looking for lights marking the end of the channel. It had been two days since he had slept, and the fatigue seemed as big a menace as the rocks. In the gray dawn, he spotted Isla de los Estados and ran to check his charts. Garside noticed charts for the area were littered with x's marking shipwrecks, and it looked as if he were about to become another one. The only way to avoid that fate was to break the seal on the engine. He had come practically all the way around the world, only to be disqualified because he needed to use his engine. He reluctantly sent a short e-mail explaining the situation to Mark Schrader.

"Will I be disqualified if I break the seal on my engine?"

Garside was lucky that Schrader happened to check his electronic mailbox in Punta del Este just ten minutes later. Schrader sent a message asking Garside if he could anchor. Garside replied, too deep, right up to shore.

As Garside waited on Schrader's OK, the boat drifted closer to the rocks. He didn't think he could wait any longer. Another few minutes and *Magellan* could be impaled. He would have to break the seal.

Suddenly, the wind blew out a small puff and the boat began to pull away. And then, Schrader's message arrived: Break the seal. You won't be disqualified, but might get a small time

penalty. Amazed at his luck, Garside rode the fickle wind out of the Straits of Le Maire.

Off the coast of Argentina a few days later, the Class Two boats were pelted by a storm that slowed their pace to a crawl. Violent headwinds shredded one of Brad Van Liew's foresails and ripped at J.P. Mouligne's rigging. It felt as if they would never shake the bad weather. Garside closed to within fifty miles of Mouligne. On paper, *Magellan* was faster than Mouligne's boat, *Cray Valley*, but the advantage had yet to show up on the race course. Mouligne's seven-day lead gnawed at Garside.

Garside and Van Liew noticed, however, that they were gaining on Mouligne only because he had slowed down. Of more concern, Mouligne had not sent an e-mail in more than a day. Wild scenarios ran through the skippers' minds. Mouligne could have hit his head or fallen overboard. The boat, under autopilot, would continue sailing.

Garside and Mouligne had a rocky relationship. Mouligne was upset early in the race when Garside called him a "frog" in an e-mail. An intense rivalry sprouted. They talked very little. Still, Garside was worried about Mouligne. He decided to break computer silence. The message was simple.

"You don't have to tell us any secrets, but let me know you're all right," Garside wrote.

On board *Cray Valley*, Mouligne was frustrated. The wind changed direction and speed every hour. He went from a gennaker - a hybrid sail, part genoa, part spinnaker - and a full mainsail to three reefs in the main and a partially rolled staysail inside of two hours. Over a twenty-four hour period, he averaged four knots. When he read the message from Garside, he was touched.

"I really knew he meant it," Mouligne recalled later. "I knew my safety was a concern to him, because his safety is to me. We depend on each other and it creates a bond that goes beyond the competitive aspects."

Mouligne sent Garside back a warm note, thanking him. He was fine and would see him in Punta.

The South American night was fading to blue on March 3 as *FILA*'s illuminated mainsail appeared on the horizon off Punta like a fat, triangular moon. Pushed along at fifteen knots by a South Atlantic breeze, the white yacht glided across the Rio de la Plata, leaving chase boats in its wake. Soldini aimed for the line of high-rise buildings twinkling on the coast. Beyond them was the Leg Three finish line.

Soldini ran around on deck in a white t-shirt, adjusting his rigging and trying to find out what was wrong with his autopilot. It had frozen up at a bad time; Soldini needed to go below to read charts of the area. The water was getting shallow and a helicopter hovered just above the mast. Three boats rocked in the water ten yards off the port stern, filming his arrival and transmitting it live on Italian television. As *FILA* approached the shore, the swells almost pitched one of the television crew boats into its port side deck spreader. Watching the feeding frenzy, Mark Schrader stewed. He would have a talk with the television people later.

Soldini arrives first at Punta del Este

It was tough sailing for Soldini. As he approached the finish line, he had to stay in the narrow channel of deep water then tack to port at the last minute to avoid a huge stone breaker that protected the yacht basin from the tides. Just before *FILA* crossed the finish line, Isabelle Autissier appeared on deck and helped furl a foresail. Race officials ignored the aid, Dan Mc-Connell said, because of extenuating circumstances: Soldini

had his hands full dodging media boats, and they were only yards from the finish. Autissier merely helped avoid a crash.

When the boat crossed the line, Schrader jumped from the Zodiac chase boat onto *FILA*'s deck. First he hugged Autissier and then Soldini, who had already gone below deck and changed into a *FILA* crew shirt. Soldini had won his second leg victory in a row after 25 days and nearly 10 hours at sea. And he still had a time credit coming for Autissier's rescue.

Nearly 500 people crowded the docks at the Punta del Este Yacht Club to watch Soldini and Autissier make landfall. They had arrived before six o'clock. Soldini was awestruck by the roaring crowd, and repeatedly threw his head into his hands as he giggled and turned red. It was the biggest welcoming committee the race had ever seen. Schrader, Autissier, and Soldini chased each other around *FILA*'s deck, spraying one another with champagne. Autissier ran so fast she slipped and fell.

Waiting at the yacht club were more than 100 foreign journalists and television crews. Reporters pushed and shoved one another for a better look. The Italian ambassador to Uruguay and a few local politicians, in full military uniform, stood behind the table where Soldini and Autissier would sit. When they walked in, reporters gave the pair a standing ovation. One television reporter even gave Autissier a bouquet of flowers.

For an hour, Soldini and Autissier recounted their Southern Ocean odyssey. And then, Autissier stunned the crowd with an announcement: She would never race around the world alone again. No more Around Alones, no more Vendee Globes. Enough was enough.

"I knew it was going to be my last Around Alone, but I did not want to say anything to anybody. I just wanted to be in the race," Autissier said. "I think it's time for me to do something else. I had ten wonderful years, but now I think it's done."

For the next few days, reporters stalked Soldini and Autissier through the South American resort town. It was not at all what the racers had come to expect from Punta del Este, which is usually the most relaxed stopover of the Around Alone. With the Southern Ocean behind them, the skippers hung around and went out together like high school seniors spending their last May together. The trip back to Charleston, they hoped, would not be as difficult as what they had already been through.

A small beach town, Punta del Este sits on the southeast corner of Uruguay, where the South Atlantic and Rio de la Plata meet. It is the French Riveria or Palm Beach of South America, and looks much like the beachfront outside of San Juan, Puerto Rico. Aside from high-rise hotels and condominiums, the coast is dotted with the beach homes of wealthy Argentines. In Punta, dinner starts around ten o'clock. The bars stay open and full until sunrise. At the tip of the town's peninsula, most of the skippers and their shore crew stay in rented homes or condos, walking from home to the Yacht Club. By the time most of the racers made it to Punta in early March, Carnival had ended and the tourist season was over. The hot summer weather gave way to cooler temperatures in the low eighties.

But Soldini didn't have a chance to relax and enjoy it. He had interviews lined up for every waking hour of the day. In between, he shuffled through charts and weather forecasts, calculating how much time he lost during the rescue. Schrader brought in an international jury to give Soldini a time compensation. Normally the race committee handled such chores, but this time wanted to avoid any further controversy. Soldini argued with the jury that he was due forty hours. They gave him twenty-four.

It was the politic thing to do - it afforded Soldini every hour he spent diverted, but did not credit him for weather patterns. Soldini made a gracious public statement and thanked the jury, then left the building with his shore crew, cursing under his breath.

"I spent time with that jury to tell them how this story was

and how the weather was and how they cannot see that, I don't know," Soldini said the next day. "I don't need the time, I'll have fifteen days. What I really care about is that it's important to go out with a strong signal that if something like this ever happens again, people should not even ask for one second in their mind, 'What's going to happen to my race?' These people are playing with fire."

Marc Thiercelin sailed into Punta del Este on March 15. In the Falkland Islands, *SOMEWHERE*'s shore crew fitted the yacht with a sixty-foot mast for the last 1,000 miles of Leg Three. It was as big a mast as the crew could get to the Falklands, and it worked well enough; it took him only a week to sail up the coast of South America. Still, the small mast was not good enough to use on Leg Four. Thiercelin had ordered a new, larger mast, one that could be flown into Buenos Aires on a 747, then shipped down the Rio de la Plata on a boat to Punta. Thiercelin meant to win the last leg against Soldini.

Soldini and Autissier meet the press in Punta del Este

Cray Valley sails into Punta; Mouligne greets Garside at the finish

"I want to finish this race for three reasons: For sportsmanship, for my sponsor - you don't have a chance every day to be involved in a round-the-world yacht race," he said. "And I don't like to leave things in the middle. I want to finish it off."

As soon as Thiercelin arrived, reporters hammered him with questions about why he hadn't turned back to rescue Autissier. Was his gooseneck damage really too bad to turn around? How had he managed to keep sailing more than 300 miles a day with a busted boom? Was there bad blood between him and Autissier? He refused to answer the questions, saying he would only talk to Soldini and Autissier about it.

A few days after he arrived, Thiercelin walked into Mark Schrader's office. For more than an hour behind a closed door, the two men talked about what had happened after Autissier capsized. Schrader still was unclear on what Thiercelin had done, and why. He had heard only from *SOMEWHERE*'s shore crew. He wanted answers. Thiercelin could not deflect questions from Schrader as easily as he had the media.

Later that afternoon, Schrader and Thiercelin issued a joint statement. Schrader did not mince words. Thiercelin had made errors in judgment and communications.

"I reminded him that doing all one can to help others in distress at sea is the cardinal rule. Singlehanders are more aware of that than most, and as a very experienced sailor he should stay more focused on that tenet in the future."

Quokka Sports, which produced the official Around Alone Web site, printed Thiercelin's remarks under the headline "Mea Culpa." In his statement, which included an apology to Soldini and Autissier, Thiercelin admitted that he was wrong. Not turning around was a mistake.

"Knowing what I do now, I realize I made two errors to which my tiredness, the communications with my shore crew and the conditions contributed greatly," he said. "First, I should have confirmed the situation personally with the ROC before proceeding to Cape Horn. And, I should have tried to heave-to until the rescue had been accomplished or I had been formally released from my station by Race Operations. . . . I now know that had I been communicating directly with Race Operations Center in Charleston, I would have immediately stopped and waited for instructions on how I could have helped. I deeply regret that I did not do so."

The rest of the fleet arrived by the end of the month in varying states of physical and mental health. Brad Van Liew was still beat up from the Southern Ocean with scars across his knuckles. Mouligne and Garside greeted him as if he were their pesky kid brother. Viktor Yazykov sailed into port almost out of drinking water. Minoru Saito's sails were in tatters. And Australian skipper Neil Hunter, the last official skipper still in the race, arrived sporting half a beard. He left his starboard side hairy to protect him from the frigid Antarctic winds blowing from the south; he shaved his port side to let the sun over South America tan him. He called it the Cape Horn cut. Hunter was sailing the slowest boat in the fleet, but he had made it. To avoid rough weather, he sailed farther north than the rest of the fleet. On Leg Three, he logged 8,600 nautical miles, 2,500 more than the rest of the fleet.

Reaching Punta del Este from the sea appears easy by the charts. The South Atlantic meets the wide mouth of the Rio de la Plata just south of the city and the Uruguay harbor is a wide, normally calm expanse of blue water. It is deceptive scenery. The water shallows quickly as the continental shelf rushes up to the beach. A boat can go from relatively deep - and safe - water to surf in less than a mile

Many of the skippers would have trouble making it into port safely. As J.P. Mouligne neared the finish line on Sunday March 7, his autopilot was broken. As he sailed toward land, he had to scramble below deck to check his charts, then run back and catch the tiller before the boat crash-jibed.

It was exhausting work, especially since he couldn't remember when he'd last slept. As Mouligne approached the breakwater separating the yacht club from the Rio de la Plata, race officials and his wife, Kate, screamed from the Zodiac chase boat for him to tack. *Cray Valley* was headed straight for the breakwater. Mouligne turned at the last minute, gunwale in the water as the boat crossed the finish line. Mouligne had not been able to leave the tiller to adjust the boat's water ballast. He had nearly capsized the boat carrying his wife.

Fifteen hours later, Mike Garside almost hit the breakwater, too, unable to distinguish the channel markers from the background lights of hotels and casinos on the horizon. As *Magellan Alpha* steamed toward the rock breakwater, Schrader screamed over the radio, "*Magellan* tack. Mike!"

As dangerous as it is to sail into Punta at night when it is calm, storms made the harbor almost impassable. Which is why race officials could not believe their tracking equipment on Saturday, March 28 when it appeared that Fedor Konioukhov was sailing straight for the beach, pushed by a 45-knot tailwind.

The Russian, disqualified after two legs, had continued to sail more or less with the fleet. He had meandered through the Southern Pacific near Hunter for much of the leg, once reporting that a dolphin had jumped into the cockpit with him. Now, with his unpredictable, erratic sailing, Konioukhov was still giving Mark Schrader headaches.

Konioukhov's son, Oscar, had told Schrader that Konioukhov would wait until late Sunday evening to arrive, when a Russian camera crew would be set up to film the finish of

the leg. But that night a gale hit *Modern University for the Humanities*. After forty days at sea, Konioukhov had had enough. He steered for the coast. Soon he was making eight knots, a quick clip for the Russian.

Race officials watched Konioukhov, scratching their heads. Schrader said he would never try to sail into a shallow harbor in those conditions. Afraid Konioukhov would run aground, he called local authorities. But they had already met the Russian adventurer.

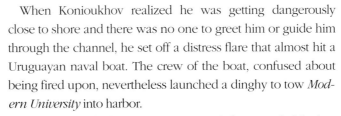

Magellan Alpha in the Rio de la Plata

When Konioukhov realized he was getting dangerously close to shore and there was no one to greet him or guide him through the channel, he set off a distress flare that almost hit a Uruguayan naval boat. The crew of the boat, confused about being fired upon, nevertheless launched a dinghy to tow *Modern University* into harbor.

Still under sail, the Russian navigated the crowded harbor and marina before docking so fast he cracked his bowsprit against the dock. By the time he got off the boat he was angry and a nervous wreck. His English improved as he cursed at Schrader.

Konioukhov wanted to know why the race committee had not met him offshore.

Schrader said he would have, but he was told the skipper wouldn't come in until Sunday.

Konioukhov ended the argument with an unmistakable, international symbol. He pointed his middle finger skyward.

Later, Konioukhov apologized to Schrader and announced that he would sail back to Charleston with the rest of the Around Alone fleet, officially or not.

Van Liew sails back into Punta del Este under jury rig.

INTO THE WIND

Racing To Charleston

CHAPTER TWENTY TWO

After the skippers left Punta del Este, most steered north into a stiff headwind. Neal Petersen went south. He took down his mainsail and let the smaller staysail move the boat along. For two days, it looked as if he were sailing back to his native South Africa.

Petersen was an emotional and physical wreck. Water from his boat's ballast tank was leaking into the bilge, and he had to pump 150 gallons overboard every hour. Like Isabelle Autissier and J.P. Mouligne, he sometimes got seasick, especially after the start of a race when his nerves were still jangled from all the pre-start festivities and his body wasn't yet conditioned to the rocking ocean swells.

But Petersen's dark mood stemmed from something deeper than seasickness or faulty equipment. He and his girlfriend of nearly eight years, Gwen Wilkinson, were having problems. In Punta del Este, she told him things weren't working out. She needed a break from him and a rest from the race.

Petersen was devastated. Wilkinson had been by his side for so long, helping him prepare for the 1994-95 race, moving to Charleston with him after his yacht was dismasted during that race's second leg. In Charleston, she lived with him on his cramped yacht, surviving the city's miserably hot summers without air conditioning or an easily accessible shower. She

had helped him form a nonprofit foundation for kids. Without her, he knew he wouldn't have made it so far.

They had met in Ireland in 1992 after a fishing boat found Petersen, injured and starving, on his boat drifting off the Irish coast. In some ways, they seemed an unlikely pair. Petersen was an idealistic and outgoing man - a cheerleader who clearly enjoyed the spotlight. Wilkinson, a pretty, petite brunette with a dry wit, was more introverted. Petersen was a blazing afternoon sun; she was Irish mist. Sometimes, Wilkinson thought the sun was just too bright. She felt uncomfortable when Petersen mentioned her in e-mail updates posted on the race's Web site. The Around Alone's stopovers were especially difficult on their relationship. Because his boat was usually one of the last ones to make it in, he had just a week or two to get ready for the next leg. That period was jammed with race functions, interviews and boat repairs. Not much quality time.

Petersen hoped to patch things up, and she had left that door open. But the day of Leg Four's restart, she had already flown back to Ireland.

"The sailing has been relatively easy compared to the emotional trials that we've had to deal with," Petersen said one night shortly after leaving Uruguay. "The race takes nine months. No other event puts people in isolation for so long

Preparing a new mast for *Balance Bar.*

and throws so many things at them - not just the skippers but the people on the shore as well. Sometimes I think of all the things that Diana Mitchell had to deal with when Harry Mitchell never came home. Isabelle's family must have gone through some very tough times as well. We tend to focus on the sailors and forget about the people we leave behind. It's like a motorcar race. The public watches and sees a crash and everyone says, 'That's exciting, did you see that crash,' but they never see the people at the hospital waiting to find out what the doctor says."

After two days, Petersen pulled himself together, hoisted the mainsail, and turned north into a brutal gale that had been pounding the fleet ever since it left Uruguay. "I just want this leg to be over," he said in an e-mail to the ROC. He was well on his way to accomplishing his dream of completing the Around Alone, but it didn't seem as satisfying now that he couldn't share it with Gwen.

High winds and choppy seas kept the fleet from speeding away from Punta del Este, and the skippers fought for every mile. Each one took a different path, and on maps in the ROC, their courses looked like a nine-legged spider. But Brad Van Liew welcomed the headwinds. His boat was faster upwind than those of his rivals, Mike Garside and J.P. Mouligne. Van Liew knew he couldn't beat Mouligne's overall time, but he was only ten hours behind Garside and still had a chance at claiming second place in the race's Class Two division. Van Liew half-jokingly vowed not to sleep on this leg. He would work his sails twenty-four hours a day to stay ahead.

On April 11, with three reefs in his mainsail, Van Liew was in his cabin, waiting for a vicious squall to die down. "I'm sick of rough weather," he said to himself while wedged into his nav station. He had seen enough of it in the Southern Ocean.

Suddenly, he felt *Balance Bar* surf down a ten-foot wave and fall into what he later described as a "pothole in the water." At the bottom of this wave, *Balance Bar* landed on its side, and Van Liew heard something snap. He still didn't believe anything was wrong. But when he looked out the window over his nav station, he was dumbfounded. The mast was gone. A shroud holding up the mast had parted, then the mast itself had broken in three places and fallen overboard. With a thud, the boom fell to the deck, and the sea swallowed his new mainsail, staysail and genoa. He scrambled onto the deck, and for two hours cut lines, rods, and rigging. His stomach churned. His race, he thought, was over.

He called the ROC and then his wife, Meaghan. He told them the rig was gone, and that he was going to break the seal on his engine and motor back to Punta. But Van Liew's wife and friends begged him not to start the engine. It would disqualify him. He couldn't give up; they would find a way to get him back in the race. When Marc Thiercelin heard what happened, he offered the mast he used to sail from the Falklands to Uruguay and an old sail. Alan Nebauer, Van Liew's shore manager, canceled his flight home, as did Phil Lee, Mouligne's shore crew leader.

Van Liew was skeptical about continuing in the race. Still, he began to fashion a jury rig. He took his twenty-foot spinnaker pole and hoisted it with some lines, running them around winches so he could control the tension on the pole. He rigged halyards that would allow him to raise and lower a storm jib and trysail. Then, he turned the boat around.

"Position is about 51.7 miles from Punta, making 4 knots," Van Liew said in message to the ROC. "I am jury-rigged and proceeding to Punta. I will try to figure out something in the way of a mast when I get there. Please advise all in the fleet I wish them a safe and enjoyable last leg."

He sounded like a man ready to quit.

Two days later, Van Liew sailed back into Punta del Este, where he was met by his wife, mother, and the shore crews of *Balance Bar, Cray Valley, SOMEWHERE* and *FILA*. They vowed to have Van Liew back in the race within the week. "When he arrived, he was sad, tired and angry," Van Liew's wife said. "But he also had a gleam in his eye about the possibilities."

Thiercelin's spare mast would not fit *Balance Bar*, but Hall Spars in Argentina could build him a new aluminum mast in thirty hours. Van Liew's wife talked to officials with Balance Bar, and they agreed to match any contributions that Van Liew's team could raise. The Conrad Resort and Casino in Punta del Este chipped in, as did members of the Punta del Este Yacht Club.

Eight days after losing its mast, *Balance Bar* was back on the water, still in contention for third place.

Leg Four was supposed to be the easy one: Cruise up the coast of South America, skirt the doldrums, keep the Caribbean to port, and then hit the trade winds to Charleston. Race director Mark Schrader said that in the previous four races every skipper who started the fourth leg had finished. Within a few days the weather did its best to prove Schrader wrong.

Short, steep seas and gusting headwinds hounded the skippers until they passed the eastern bulge of Brazil. Almost everyone was miserable. Several skippers had colds, others were seasick. Even J.P. Mouligne's luck appeared to be running out. He had won the first three legs by impressive margins. He sidestepped windless holes while others fell into them. He was even greeted by a rainbow when he sailed into Cape Town. But now, he couldn't seem to catch Garside, who except for taking out a hunk off his toe during a crash jibe, was making all the right moves. Worse, heavy winds had ripped Mouligne's mainsail. And his knee, which he tried to ignore, was hurting terribly. By April 18, it had swollen to the

size of a grapefruit and turned a blistering pink. He phoned Dr. Dan Carlin, the fleet's physician. Carlin couldn't make a good diagnosis without seeing the knee. No problem, Mouligne said. He took out his digital camera, took a few snapshots, and e-mailed them to Quokka Sports, the company that produced the Around Alone Web site. They, in turn, e-mailed the photos to Carlin in Boston.

Mouligne didn't like the prognosis Carlin sent back. The knee was infected, and if it spread, Mouligne might have to be airlifted off his yacht. His race would be over. Carlin directed Mouligne to take some antibiotics, stay off the knee, and keep his leg elevated. Mouligne took the medicine, but instead of resting, he worked through the night, stitching Kevlar patches to his tattered mainsail.

Two days later, he sent an e-mail to the ROC: "The last two days have been the most frustrating of my life. My knee is doing much better and the swelling has come down a lot. The mainsail also looks as if it is going to hold. It is now a matter of sailing smart, and catching up. With 4,000 miles to go, I have time and cannot get discouraged."

With an eight-day lead in the Class Two race, Mouligne was almost guaranteed to win his division. But he wanted to do what only two other skippers had done before: sweep all four legs in his class. With Garside pulling away, Mouligne knew he would have to be sharp for the rest of the race.

For the next week, Mouligne would fight back into contention only to see Garside go streaking off once again, leaving *Cray Valley* deep in his wake. On April 28, a large black bird landed on *Cray Valley*'s deck. "I am not a big fan of birds, and I am also superstitious, so this bird did not look good to me at all," Mouligne said in an e-mail. "As a matter of fact, as soon as the bird was on the boat, the wind died completely."

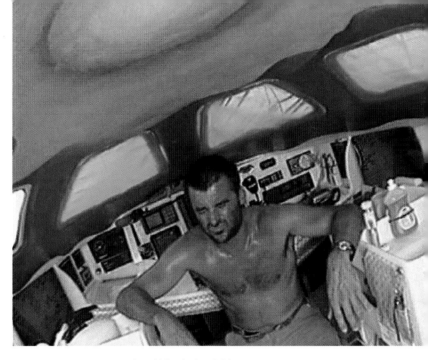

Cray Valley in the doldrums

Mike Garside's *Magellan Alpha*

Closing The Circle

CHAPTER TWENTY THREE

After 21,000 miles of storms, rescues, and splintered masts, the final 6,000 miles to Charleston could have had as much suspense as a trip to the grocery store. When the fleet left Punta del Este, Giovanni Soldini was twelve days ahead of Marc Thiercelin in Class One, and J.P. Mouligne had an eight-day lead over Mike Garside in Class Two. But Leg Four would end up being a dramatic contest unto itself. Even more than their windblown journeys across the Southern Ocean, the dash to the finish line would show what kind of stuff the Around Alone skippers were made of.

In Uruguay, Thiercelin made it clear he was ready for a fight. He had almost no chance of winning the overall race, but with the help of his sponsor, he spent tens of thousands of dollars to have a new mast sent to Punta del Este so he would be competitive with Soldini. A duel between the two seemed a fitting finale. From the beginning, Soldini had been put off by Thiercelin's attitude that the Around Alone was merely a warmup to the French Vendee Globe. Thiercelin's decision not to turn toward Isabelle Autissier's capsized boat and his criticism of her performance only stirred the pot. Meanwhile, Thiercelin felt he was wrongly cast as the race's bad boy. "The finish will be the most intense part of the race," he said the day before the fleet left Uruguay.

The Class Two rivalry between Mouligne and Garside was just as passionate, though it had grown friendlier over time. Not only did they joust on the water, they played mind games with each other in cyberspace. Shortly after the fleet left Punta del Este, Mouligne sent an e-mail saying his stove had broken. Garside promptly zapped one back talking about "the best piece of barbecued Uruguayan beef and twelve freshest eggs I have ever had. J.P., my supper was out of this world last night. Piping hot chicken with boiled rice and gravy. And I'm really looking forward to my tortellini con prosciutto di Parma e parmigiana reggiano tonight." On April 24, when his lead had grown to more than 200 miles, Garside wrote a more serious note: "We are both nursing damaged boats and bodies. I suppose we could both take it easy now as our first and second places are almost guaranteed as long as we cross the finish line. But that's not in my nature, and I don't think it's in J.P.'s either. I desperately want to win this leg. I've wanted to win them all, but if I can take this one, I will join Mike Golding as the only Brits to have won a leg of this race."

In the back of the fleet, skippers who had no real chance of winning any of the legs burned with the same competitive fire. Neal Petersen and Minoru Saito had an especially spirited rivalry, with Petersen crowing in an e-mail April 29 that he was able "to cut the corner and get around the top of Brazil, pulling many miles on Minoru and regaining my lead." They would trade places for the rest of the leg.

Even Robin Davie, who had been disqualified, was enjoying a race with Brad Van Liew. Van Liew's dismasting had given Davie a chance to catch up. "I'm sure the fact that both of us are heading up the line together will keep us on our toes and make for a faster passage to Charleston," Davie said in a message to the ROC. "You can't have two boats sailing together to the same place without it becoming a race."

In mid-April, as Soldini moved into the doldrums, he spent hours at his computer surfing the Web for the latest forecasts. It was a critical time in the leg. Some parts of the windless doldrums were expanding while other areas were contracting. The narrow stretches were like doors. Get through one quickly and he wouldn't lose too much time; miss one and he might get stuck for days. As Soldini sped north, he found four different forecasts. Three predicted that the narrowest area would be to the west, toward the Brazilian coast. That's the door, Soldini thought. If he could get far enough west in time, the door might slam shut and trap Thiercelin, who was just ninety miles behind.

When not at his computer, Soldini spent time on *FILA*'s deck making sure the boat was properly rigged. His boom had cracked near the boom vang, and he marked the crack with a pen to measure any increase. It seemed okay, though, and as the temperature rose, Soldini felt more and more loose. He tried to avoid flying too many sails or changing sail configurations. "The boat goes better when it's not swamped in sails," he said in a message. "And the time you make up in the short term is often lost at the end because you make mistakes when you're rushing."

As he crossed the equator, his lead over Thiercelin dwindled to sixty-two miles. Temperatures rose to one hundred degrees.

The sails hung like limp rags. A strong ocean current ran against the boat, and *FILA* chugged along at less than four knots. Soldini feared that his French rival would catch up.

But his decision to head west proved to be the right one. The light winds lasted for just one day. Suddenly, the door opened, and trade winds filled the boat's sails. *FILA* streaked north at a twelve-knot clip and within a few days was more than 400 miles ahead of Thiercelin. Soldini sent a message: "I broke the rules a bit: I allowed myself three glasses of red wine! I think I've deserved it."

Meanwhile, to the east, Thiercelin's boat *SOMEWHERE* sailed as if stuck to flypaper. "No wind, no wind," Thiercelin said in an e-mail to the ROC on April 25. For two days, the sea was as flat as a prairie, and like a charcoal sketch, heavy rain made the sky and water blend into sad shades of gray and white. From the daily reports, he watched Soldini take off. "Rain, rain, rain, and no wind. I see Leg Four going on and me staying here. This is a bad, bad time for me. The race is finished."

Just after 1 a.m. May 8, on a moonless night off the coast of Charleston, Soldini steered toward buoys seven and eight, the Around Alone finish line. Despite the hour, a fleet of forty boats streamed out of the harbor to greet him, their twinkling lights making the water a mirror image of the starry sky. As Soldini neared the end of his adventure, he thought about Andrea Romanelli, his friend who had been swept overboard a year before. Romanelli had helped him build the boat, and Soldini still felt his presence. Sometimes he could hear Andrea saying, "C'mon, Giovanni," and, "What are you doing?" Soldini was about to win the race, and he felt a deep sense of satisfaction. All the work that Romanelli had put into it paid off.

Soon, several boats filled with photographers and television camera operators slid into FILA's wake. They pointed spotlights at the boat, illuminating its sails, and from a distance, *FILA* looked like a giant lamp on a black tablecloth. A shooting

star streaked across the sky, and a steady breeze pushed *FILA* over the line at 1:32 a.m.

Then came the noise. Charleston native Ned Stender fired a blast from an old Civil War cannon mounted on the back of his nineteen-foot Whaler. Horns from the spectator fleet blared, and people screamed and whistled. Three pink flares arced over *FILA*'s mast. Soldini ignited a bright white flare and jumped up and down on the deck.

Soldini's elapsed time for the race was 116 days, 20 hours, and 8 minutes - four days better than the record set in 1990-91 by Christophe Auguin. Soldini also was the first non-French sailor to win the race.

Race organizers towed Soldini to the City Marina. More than 300 spectators and friends were waiting, so many that the marina's floating docks began to sink. Race officials handed Soldini a giant bottle of Champagne. He uncorked it and sprayed it on his shore crew. "I can't believe so many people came out at four o'clock to see me," he said. Someone asked what he was going to do next.

"I'm going to party."

Six hours later, more than a hundred people gave him a standing ovation when he walked into the auditorium of Mason Prep School for a press conference. Soldini sat at a folding table on a stage; his shoulders were hunched but his feet were planted wide and flat on the floor. He looked relaxed and at peace as he spoke about his friend Romanelli. "I am very glad that this race went so well, so everyone can appreciate the work Andrea did. The boat was his child." Then he thanked his shore crew, Claudia Palisi, Bruno Laurent, Guido Broggi and Yves Dupasquier. "We won the race much more on land than on the sea. During the two legs in the Southern Ocean, we never had any problems with the boat, and that is the real

key." He added that the race had changed him. "It's a long period. You see things. You grow." He was thrilled with his victory, but he had learned during the past year that "winning is no big deal. The important thing is to be with your crew, your family, to wake up in the morning and be happy."

For many skippers and their families and shore crews, the fifth edition of the Around Alone was a destructive and emotional event. All sixteen spent years - even decades - preparing for the race, and almost half saw their dreams dashed in one way or another. Three boats lost their masts, two skippers retired because of equipment problems, two others were disqualified, another skipper ran aground, one boat capsized. Unlike the 1986 and 1994 races, no one was lost at sea - though there were many close calls: Josh Hall was nearly washed

Soldini crosses finish line in Charleston.

Thiercelin finishes

overboard one dark night. Thiercelin's mast crashed through the cabin roof, missing his head by inches. Van Liew and Petersen endured violent knockdowns near Cape Horn. Viktor Yazykov survived a dangerous infection - and his own creative first aid techniques. Autissier survived a capsize in the world's most remote ocean.

Despite all this destruction, the Around Alone was a platform for some truly remarkable sailing. In 1967, Sir Francis Chichester sailed around the world in 226 days, averaging 126 miles per day. Thirty-two years later, Soldini ticked off an average of 230 miles per day. On several occasions, Soldini, Thiercelin and Autissier all nearly broke the 400-mile-per-day barrier. In fact, because of advances in boat designs, the limiting factor on even higher speeds "is no longer technology, but the human element," said Claudio Stampi, a Harvard researcher who studied the skippers' sleep patterns. Successful skippers are those who know when to push and when to sail conservatively - sailors who know their own emotional and physical limits. Long-distance singlehanded sailing may be considered an "extreme" sport, but the top skippers are models of moderation. Despite Soldini's outwardly cavalier personality and his reputation for making wild gambles in choosing routes, he was the one who first noticed a potentially dangerous storm south of the Kerguelen Islands in the second leg - a move that resulted in the fleet agreeing to stay north of the islands. During the third leg, when Autissier went far south toward a region of higher winds and icebergs, Soldini stayed north where the winds weren't so strong. Stampi said Soldini seemed to be attuned to his body's needs and rhythms, taking naps before he became too fatigued, keeping enough

energy in reserve for emergencies. For instance, before Soldini set off on his mission to rescue Autissier, he had slept nearly six hours, enabling him to sail the next thirty-two hours without sleep. "Giovanni did the best job of managing his emotional and physical energy and resources," Mark Schrader said. "He knows what's important in life and what's not, and he's a pretty young guy to have figured that out."

Thiercelin would conclude his race the same way he spent much of it: Frustrated. A day-and-a-half after Soldini won, Thiercelin tacked a zigzag course to the finish line. *SOMEWHERE* inched along on a carpet of gently undulating swells. The wind was somewhere else.

His last week at sea was miserable. After Soldini beat him through the doldrums, a squall finished him off, knocking his yacht on its side and turning his sails into a tangled mess. As he sorted out everything, a loose line wrapped around the rudder shaft. While jury-rigging a preventer, he fell off the boom and landed on his back. He took painkillers for the rest of the leg. In Charleston, Thiercelin declared the Around Alone tougher than the Vendee Globe.

He added that he wanted to work on his communication skills to prevent future misunderstandings such as the controversy over Autissier's rescue. But he defended his silence on the water. He preferred solitude when sailing and hated the intrusive effects of the Internet and satellite phones on solo racing. Still, Thiercelin said he wanted to do it again. "If I do well, maybe my sponsor will allow me to do the next Around Alone in four years."

Over the next three weeks, the rest of the fleet would trickle across the finish line. Mike Garside, the British skipper who hated sailing, would battle Mouligne up the Atlantic and finally win one of the race's legs. Because of his exceptional performance in the first three legs, Mouligne nevertheless won Class Two by a wide margin. His focus and determination on the water and his skill and ease with the international media put him in a solid position for sponsorship in future races.

Yazykov would have another triumphant leg. Eight months before, he had started the race injured and depressed, but the longer he was at sea, the more trials he faced, the stronger and happier he seemed to get. By the end, he was all smiles, proud of the boat he built himself in his small hometown on the Black Sea, satisfied that he had finally realized his childhood dream of sailing around the world alone.

At first, Van Liew would be deeply disappointed that his broken mast knocked him out of contention in Leg Four. But after leaving Uruguay with a new rig, he stormed back up the coast and passed some of the slower boats, all the way buoyed by the knowledge that his fellow skippers and their shore crews had made it possible for him to finish something that few have done.

In his tiny home-built boat, Petersen would become the first black person to race around the world alone, silencing critics who said his boat wasn't seaworthy, or that he wasn't a good sailor. Petersen's fourth leg wasn't easy, though. Midway, he learned that much of his food was contaminated, forcing him to live on half his normal rations. His finish was bittersweet. His girlfriend would not be in Charleston to meet him. And like many of the skippers, he was in a funk about his future. After you sail around the world, what do you do for an encore?

Minoru Saito would complete his third solo circumnavigation, the first Japanese man to do so, and make good on his pre-race vow: "This time, not last boat." Along the way, he popped pills for his heart condition, and at sixty-five, was the oldest man to finish a solo circumnavigation race. Neil Hunter, sailing in the slowest boat in the fleet, would show that the tortoise still has a chance against the hares, outlasting skippers like Autissier, Hall and Mike Golding, all of whom had million-dollar yachts and big-buck corporate sponsors.

Finally, disqualified skippers Fedor Konioukhov and Robin Davie would shadow the fleet. Like Saito, Davie joined an elite group of ocean sailors who have sailed alone around the world three times. Though officially out of the race, both Konioukhov and Davie knew they were beaten by race rules, not the sea.

At 27,000 miles, the Around Alone is the longest race of any kind for an individual. Like climbing Mount Everest, the race remains a dangerous undertaking, despite advances in boat designs and communication technology. Unlike Everest, the race isn't "there." It is a man-made endeavor, and as the skippers made it back to Charleston, an uneasiness about the event's future lingered over the docks. While COMSAT Mobile Communications and several other sponsors helped pay some of the bills, the race didn't have a title sponsor. Even before the race, organizers told the skippers they didn't have enough cash to give the winners prize money, as had been done in previous races. Some observers doubted the next race's viability without a corporate benefactor.

No matter what happens to the Around Alone, the 1998-99 race was packed with dramatic stories and powerful images: The tense night of Yazykov's self surgery; Mike Golding's pained expression after his boat ran aground; Autissier's capsize and Soldini's heroic charge to rescue her; the exhilarating spectacle of sailboats gracefully humming through mountainous waves at the bottom of the world.

For the skippers, the race was a chance to test themselves. In doing so they forged bonds with one another that can only be understood by those who live through long periods of danger. For the rest of us, it was an eight-month lesson in courage, endurance, and living life moment-by-moment, a sea-story that showed that dreams can be as powerful as an ocean wave.

CREDITS

Robin Bass is a staff photographer for *The Post and Courier:* pages 10, 22, 34, 91, 98,108, 109, 110, 111.

Billy Black is an internationally recognized maritime photographer: Cover photo, pages 7, 14, 30, 36, 42, 43, 44, 46, 59, 60, 70, 74, 83 (PPL), 84 (PPL), 106, 116.

Carlo Borlenghi is a professional photographer and owner of the photo agency Sea & See Italia: pages 5, 88, 93, 99.

Matthew Fortner is a staff photographer for *The Post and Courier:* pages 2, 3, 6 left, 24, 48, 49, 52, 53, 54, 56.

Ricardo Figueredo Freire: page 112.

Gill Guerry is the art director for *The Post and Courier:* book design and graphics pages 41, 58, 103, 124, end papers.

Alan Hawes is a staff photographer for *The Post and Courier:* pages 8, 9, 11, 13, 119.

Paula Illingworth is a Charleston-based freelance photographer: page 6 right.

Bill Jordan is a staff photographer for *The Post and Courier:* page 12.

Ian Mainsbridge/Nokia/PPL: page X, 62.

J.P. Mouligne: page 16, 115 (courtesy of quokka.com).

Brad Nettles is a staff photographer for *The Post and Courier:* pages 18, 19.

Mark Pepper is a photographer based in England: pages 23, 66, 68, 69.

Laszlo Pal is an Emmy-award winning filmmaker: bottom of pages 38, 39.

National Oceanic and Atmospheric Administration: page 20.

Neal Petersen: page 104.

PPL is a British picture agency: X, 62, 83, 84.

Mic Smith is a staff photographer for *The Post and Courier:* pages 26, 28, 120.

Wade Spees is a staff photographer for *The Post and Courier:* pages 4, 25, 47, 37, 47, 50, 73, 75, 76, 78, 79, 80, 82, 86, 105.

Jacques Vapillon is an internationally recognized maritime photographer: pages 87, 90.

Brad Van Liew: pages 94, 97, 100.

Meaghan Van Liew: page 114.

ACKNOWLEDGEMENTS

The authors would like to express their thanks to the sixteen Around Alone skippers. While under great time constraints, many freely and patiently shared their thoughts and experiences. Without their help, this book would not have been possible. Their families and shore crews, especially Phil and Robin Lee, Ned Stender, Bill Scott, Oscar Konioukhov, Kathy Stark, Meaghan Van Liew, Tracy Hughes, and Claire Lewis were extremely helpful and kind. Thanks also to race organizers Mark Schrader and Dan McConnell for their insights and patience, and the guys in the Charleston ROC, Pete Dunning, George Fenwick, Burt Irlich, Ron Magliacane, and Quinn Olsen. Additional thanks to Michelle Blockley, Jane McConnell, Polly Gatehouse, Jane Tuttle, Loretta Baxter, Donna Spears and Robbie Freeman.

Herb McCormick, who co-authored the first book on The BOC Challenge, *Out There*, wrote excellent pieces throughout the race for his magazine *Cruising World* and the race's Web site, and offered us vital guidance. Dan Miller, another race official, helped facilitate photographs and supplied many other details, and provided the invaluable service of waking us up in the middle of the night to go out and meet the boats as they neared the finish lines. Emmy-award winning filmmaker Laszlo Pal of PAL Productions in Seattle, who is producing the documentary *Around Alone - 1998-99*, supplied exciting images. Thanks also to WCIV-Charleston for assisting us with technical issues.

A number of freelance photographers and their assistants helped us sort out the book's dramatic images, including Billy Black, Joyce Tickel, Robin De Lafuente, Jacques Vapillon, Sea & See Italia, Mark Pepper, and PPL in Great Britain. The race's Web site, produced by Quokka Sports, was Internet journalism at its best. COMSAT Mobile Communications, the race's sponsor, allowed us to use its amazing satellite network to reach the skippers on several occasions.

In Auckland, New Zealand, Peter Rachtman made sure our stay was informative and productive. Thanks to Graham and Janice Bougardt for taking care of us in Cape Town and to Julie Weston for driving us around in her rental car. In Punta del Este, Uruguay, author Derek Lundy imparted vast insight into the Vendee Globe and, as importantly, provided great mealtime company. Dr. Dan Carlin's input was crucial on the race's many medical issues. Finally, we wish to thank *The Post and Courier* for the time and resources to complete this project.

race scorecard

Isabelle Autissier

Class: One
Home port: La Rochelle, France
Entry nationality: France
Date of birth: October 18, 1956
Yacht: PRB
  Designer: Groupe Finot
  Length: 60'
Sponsor: PRB

Robin Davie

Class: Two
Home port: Charleston, SC
Entry nationality: USA
Date of birth: November 2, 1951
Yacht: South Carolina
  Designer: Bergstrom/Ridder
  Length: 49'
Sponsor: Yacht clubs, others

Mike Golding

Class: One
Home port: Southampton, England
Entry nationality: UK
Date of birth: August 27, 1960
Yacht: Team Group 4
  Designer: Groupe Finot
  Length: 60'
Sponsor: Group 4 Securitas

Michael Garside

Class: Two
Home port: Cambridge, England
Entry nationality: UK
Date of birth: May 16, 1944
Yacht: Magellan Alpha
  Designer: Groupe Finot
  Length: 50'
Sponsor: Magellan Line Projects Ltd.

Josh Hall

Class: One
Home port: Ipswich, England
Entry nationality: UK
Date of birth: May 18, 1962
Yacht: Gartmore Investment Mgmt.
  Designer: Groupe Finot
  Length: 60'
Sponsor: Gartmore Investment Mgmt.

Neil Hunter

Class: Two
Home port: Melbourne, Australia
Entry nationality: Australia
Date of birth: September 26, 1949
Yacht: Paladin II
  Designer: Farr
  Length: 40'
Sponsor: None

Fedor Konioukho

Class: One
Home port: Moscow, Russia
Entry nationality: Russia
Date of birth: December 12, 1951
Yacht: Modern University for the Humanities
  Designer: Harle   **Length:** 60'
Sponsor: Modern U./ Humanities

Winner - Class Two

J.P. Mouligne

Class: Two
Home port: Newport R.I., USA
Entry nationality: France
Date of birth: April 18, 1956
Yacht: Cray Valley
  Designer: Groupe Finot
  Length: 50'
Sponsor: Cray Valley

Neal
Petersen

Class: Two
Home port: Charleston, SC, USA
Entry nationality: South Africa
Date of birth: June 3, 1967
Yacht: www.no-barriers.com
   Designer: Petersen/Goulooz
   Length: 40'
Sponsor: S.C.SPA, Phillips Industrial

Sebastian
Reidl

Class: One
Home port: Vancouver, BC, Canada
Entry nationality: Canada
Date of birth: May 22, 1939
Yacht: Project Amazon
   Designer: Sponberg
   Length: 60'
Sponsor: Project Amazon

Minoru
Saito

Class: Two
Home port: Tokyo, Japan
Entry nationality: Japan
Date of birth: January 7, 1934
Yacht: Shuten-dohji II
   Designer: Adams/Radford
   Length: 50'
Sponsor: None

Giovanni
Soldini

Class: One
Home port: Milan, Italy
Entry nationality: Italy
Date of birth: May 16, 1966
Yacht: FILA
   Designer: Groupe Finot
   Length: 60'
Sponsor: FILA

George
Stricker

Class: Two
Home port: Newport, Kentucky
Entry nationality: USA
Date of birth: October 21, 1935
Yacht: Rapscallion III
   Designer: Marek
   Length: 50'
Sponsor: None

Marc
Thiercelin

Class: One
Home port: La Rochelle, France
Entry nationality: France
Date of birth: October 29, 1960
Yacht: SOMEWHERE
   Designer: Groupe Finot
   Length: 60'
Sponsor: SOMEWHERE

Brad
Van Liew

Class: Two
Home port: Los Angeles, California
Entry nationality: USA
Date of birth: February 13, 1968
Yacht: Balance Bar
   Designer: Lyons/Martin
   Length: 50'
Sponsor: Balance Bar

Viktor
Yazykov

Class: Two
Home port: Sochi, Russia
Entry nationality: Russia
Date of birth: October 29, 1948
Yacht: Wind of Change Russia
   Designer: Adams/Yazykov/Baker
   Length: 40'
Sponsor: Atlas Shipping Company

ABOUT THE AUTHORS

Tony Bartelme is a senior writer with *The Post and Courier* in Charleston, South Carolina. Bartelme covered the 1994-95 BOC Challenge and has received numerous regional and national awards for his investigative reporting. He has freelanced for international and national publications. Born in Minneapolis, Minnesota, Bartelme lives in Charleston with his wife, Paula Illingworth, and their son, Luke.

Brian Hicks is a general assignment writer with *The Post and Courier*. A former Nashville-based political reporter for *The Chattanooga Times*, Hicks' journalism has appeared in national newspapers and magazines. In 1998, he was named South Carolina Press Association Journalist of the Year. Hicks was born in Cleveland, Tennessee, and now lives in Charleston with his wife, Beth, and their son, Cole.